LIGHTNING

Jesus said, 'I saw Satan fall like lightning from heaven.
I have given you authority to trample on snakes and
scorpions, and to overcome all the power of the enemy;
nothing will harm you.'
(Luke 10:18–19)

Lightning
from Heaven

John Widdas and Peter Mockford

KINGSWAY PUBLICATIONS
EASTBOURNE

First published 1993

Unless otherwise indicated, biblical quotations are from the
New International Version © 1973, 1978, 1984 by the
International Bible Society.

ISBN 0 85476 357 0

Produced by Bookprint Creative Services
P.O. Box 827, BN23 6NX, England for
KINGSWAY PUBLICATIONS LTD
Lottbridge Drove, Eastbourne, E Sussex BN23 6NT.
Printed in Great Britain

This book is dedicated to our families,
with thanks for their support and love,
and to the Church of St Editha's
for their prayer and backing.

Acknowledgements

We would like to thank the many friends and colleagues who have assisted in the production of this book.

In particular we would like to thank the Ven G. Kuhrt, the Revd D. Peat and the Revd C. Raven.

Contents

Introduction

Admitting that one suffers from demonic attack is just about as embarrassing as admitting that one has 'BO' at a Palace garden party. Consequently very few do, and rarely do we find Christians owning up to this problem in public or in print.

We came to the realisation that we did, in fact, suffer from this form of attack. Despite the fact that we had heard little of this complaint before, it seemed difficult to believe we were some rare breed of Christian which is susceptible. When we attended services and training days elsewhere we discovered that we did not just experience these symptoms on our own patch, but in other locations as well. We made discreet enquiries and discovered that spiritual attack is fairly common in growing churches where the gospel is preached in an uncompromising manner. Those afflicted find it difficult not only to admit to it, but to know what it is.

We found it frustrating to look on and watch the devastation caused in the churches we visited. Yet no one did anything about it or commented upon it. Often not even the leaders seemed to be aware of it. We felt the time had come to speak of our experiences and of how we felt God led us to deal with the problem. We realise we will be opening ourselves to both ridicule and

attack, yet we feel the situation is so serious that we have
to bring the problem into the open. We only took this
decision to write after a great deal of prayer and heart-
searching.

The book is written 'on the hoof'. It is a statement of
where we are, and of what we have discovered to date.
We realise that our experience may be limited, but we
have consulted with others in various parts of the country
and learn from them as they experience similar oppressive
attacks.

We make reference to some of the loathsome practices
of some satanic groups, but we have not provided any
sensational disclosures of their activities which have not
been published before. Rather we describe how these
rituals appear to affect us and other members of the
church by causing oppressive symptoms. This does not
prove that human sacrifice and other horrific acts upon
people and animals take place. When, on some occasions,
we have assumed their existence during ministry,
freedom and peace have come to those with whom we
have been praying. It is usually the last option that we
take and so the release comes after a considerable period
of prayer and counselling that touch upon many other
possibilities.

Dealing with the effects of demonic attack and the
cursing of the church by those who wish us ill represents
only a small part of the whole of our parish's life and
work. We know, though, that if it is not recognised and
dealt with swiftly it would consume far more of our time
and energy, and would blight the whole of the church's
work. We wonder how many churches do suffer stoically
when simple solutions in Christ are to hand.

We have often been asked why we are subject to so
much attack. The answer seems to be that God calls each
church to particular specialisations of ministry. He allows

it so that we can learn and share what we have learnt. We in turn benefit greatly from the insights of other churches.

We talk about the problem in Tamworth simply because that is where we happen to be. This problem is widespread, in this country and elsewhere. We owe a great debt of thanks to the people of St Editha's. There is an honesty of approach here, a desire to live in the world of reality, and a mutual trust which have made it possible for us to undertake the exploration described in this book.

Many of the situations we describe in this book were of a sensitive nature. Accordingly we have not used actual names in case histories.

Peter Mockford
John Widdas

I

Cause and Effect

For a split second the farcical nature of it all was uppermost in John's mind. He and Janine were forcibly dragging a man to church! He'd often heard talk about 'dragging people to church' but had never thought they would actually be doing it.

Lionel was quite strong and so Janine and John had to pull hard on his arms. They had managed to get halfway up the path to the church door when he froze entirely with his feet locked in front of him. They could make no more progress. His whole body was shaking violently as he experienced what was clearly absolute terror. His hands were like blocks of ice, though sweat was pouring from him.

To their amazement, Lionel's eyes were fixed on the lovely medieval building. It was this that was causing him to vibrate with fear.

'I feel as if I'm going to my execution!' he shouted.

'Don't be ridiculous,' said John, and gave him an extra heave towards the door. The side chapel was nearest, so they made for that, and pitched him forward onto his knees at the communion rail.

John caught sight of the caretaker who, seeing this strange performance, scurried into a side room.

'Good,' he thought, happy that she would not be

confused or distressed by any more of Lionel's strange behaviour.

Janine knelt beside Lionel while John stood behind him to keep him at the rail. He placed his hands on Lionel's head as Janine placed hers on his shoulders and neck. John began to pray about his troubles and Janine broke into her recently discovered gift of tongues. They were a little pressed for time so John launched straight into a confused prayer to the effect that if there was any alien entity troubling Lionel, it should leave him now. Lionel's shoulders stiffened as though he was lifting an enormous weight, then he shuddered violently and let out an ear-splitting scream.

John suddenly thought of the caretaker: 'She'll think we are raving lunatics!' Then his thoughts turned to: 'Why am I here? I don't want to be here. I didn't want to get involved in all of this in the first place!'

But now his whole being seemed to be penetrated with something akin to an electric shock. It forcibly reminded him of a time when he put his fingers into a light bulb bayonet socket as a child and received a nasty surprise.

His mind did a quick 'systems check' and reported that all was not well. He had never felt quite like this before. A sense of unreality began to creep over him. He felt like a spectator on the world around, no longer actually part of it. His heart was beating as though he had run the four-minute mile. He was terrified.

Now that was strange. Both before and during the time of ministry his mood, though tinged with fear, was largely one of irritation and embarrassment at being dragged into a ministry he did not believe in. He was clear in his own mind that there was no such thing as a personification of evil and that belief in the existence of demons was hopelessly outdated. And so his prayer had been more of an attempt to use language that was expected of him than a prayer of conviction.

In just a few minutes his theology had been revised radically in the cold light of experience. Now he knew, without a shadow of a doubt, that demonic oppression can happen in the twentieth century. He had just experienced it.

Lionel brought him back from his thoughts as he declared, 'I feel fine!' John just wished he did too. Janine didn't look too well either. John wondered if that was how he looked.

Somehow he managed to mumble a concluding prayer, and they left the church. Janine was looking flushed and very determined. She had that look of a person with a mission.

'I must go and pray over the curate's baby,' she said.

Instinctively John felt this was wrong, but he couldn't be sure. In any case, what could be wrong in praying for someone? Off she went, determined to do great things.

John walked towards the road, where a cat was just crossing towards him. For all the world it looked like a tiger coming to pounce on him. He ran off in alarm and despondency.

As he walked back home he began to ponder on how they had got into this mess. And what was Janine doing to the curate's child? But he was too confused and too frightened to do anything of a positive nature. He just wanted to get home and hide. How could he have been so foolish as to get into this situation? Why had he not avoided any ministry to Lionel, and then with a bit of good fortune, it would all have just gone away? None of what had just happened made sense, but he was equally sure that, whatever it was, it was highly dangerous.

'I am a supposedly responsible church leader of many years standing in the Anglican Church, a rural dean, and a prebendary of the Cathedral,' he thought. 'What am I doing being so foolish as to allow myself to get caught up in this potentially damaging and discrediting activity?' He could well do without it.

Yet John had the ominous feeling that, like a bad cold, it would not be going away. Even then he instinctively knew that this event was challenging many of his cherished beliefs, as he felt himself being pulled towards that wing of the church which caused him to cringe with embarrassment. 'Surely I'm not going to become one of those fundamentalist "devil bashers", am I?'

He had spent six years at Kelham Theological College being trained in a conservative liberal atmosphere. Michael Ramsey was the focus of Anglicanism for him. 'What would he have made of this afternoon's capers?' he wondered.

He tried to remember what teaching had been given on this topic. Very little, as far as he could recall, but he did have to write an essay about whether we can accept that the devil really exists. At the time he felt he had been rather clever in leaving the issue open. He put the arguments for and against (more against than for, as it happened) and left it at that. It seemed to satisfy the tutor, but it certainly did not satisfy John right now.

Then had come the book by Bishop John Robinson, *Honest to God*, and as a result a more full-blooded liberalism spread throughout the church. What a breath of fresh air that had seemed at the time! John had embraced it with relish. He felt he was in the forefront of Christian thinking. It was so reasonable, and it dealt neatly with all those difficult first-century issues of demonic activity, walking on water, and producing extra loaves and fishes . It presented a way of communicating the gospel which seemed much more acceptable to the people of the day.

And yet in recent years it had been worrying him—was that 'sweet reasonableness' taking away the challenge and the sharp edge of the gospel? He was having to admit to himself that it didn't seem to attract many to the life of the church, and those who did come found it very embarrassing to talk about the things of God. Come to think of it, so did he when he wasn't in the pulpit.

John's mind raced on. Then came the time when he realised that the training at our Theological Colleges had taught little about counselling. He therefore spent a great deal of time in later years reading Jungian psychology, going on courses, and putting this thinking into practice. What a breath of fresh air that also had seemed. He now had the feeling that at least Jung would have been fascinated and not embarrassed by his experience, though he doubted if he would have accepted what was plain to John now: he had been invaded by an oppressive presence. This had not come from his unconscious; it had come from a man called Lionel.

He had hoped to undergo further training in counselling and then apply for a post as a Director of Pastoral Care and Counselling in the Anglican Church. In order to apply for one particular course, he needed to complete a hundred hours in counselling himself, so he duly signed on. That was a precious time when he learned so much about himself. So much so that he felt he really knew who and what he was at the core of his being. A change in direction seemed irrelevant. That training in looking deep within himself helped him to realise that what was happening within him now was disturbing at the deepest level. He felt in his bones that this was a serious situation which could have dangerous consequences.

In this, at least, he was right. The curate rang. He was

irate that John had 'sent' Janine round to pray with his child. How could John expose him to such danger? Clearly there was demonic activity here, and as usual, he hinted, John would not acknowledge it.

'Mercifully, we are in good shape spiritually after last week's conference,' the curate said, 'and so we know that all that she said about us being hypocrites and needing to deeply repent was nonsense.'

That night, and for several nights to come, John had little or no sleep. Every time he dozed off he had dreadful nightmares and quite untypically woke up sweating with fear.

After a week of torment he went to see Lionel.

'You have not levelled with me!' he said bluntly. 'You asked me to pray with you because you said you just could not find the Lord. Others around you were plainly enjoying the Lord's presence but you felt you had a blockage. I can now see that there was much more to the story than this. What didn't you tell me?' he asked.

Lionel began to shake and sob. 'I have been going to a satanic group,' he replied. 'I want to get away from it. It's ruining my life.'

This came as no great revelation to John. In fact he was relieved that there was a sane and logical explanation for the way Janine and he were feeling. She, meanwhile, was going round the parish on a weird prayer crusade, accusing many faithful church members of hypocrisy and sin. They were all going into paroxysms of repentance, mixed with confusion as to what they were actually repenting about. What seemed, at first sight, to be a genuine conviction from the Lord became questionable as no good seemed to be coming from it.

John returned home and rang the Diocesan Adviser for the Ministry of Deliverance. He reminded John that in a few days they would both be at the Diocesan Clergy

Conference. During the first break in the conference programme they went for a long walk and John poured out the whole confusing story. They then retired to a room in the conference centre and the Adviser prayed for John's deliverance from a spirit of fear. The cloud lifted, he came back to the world of reality, and the palpitations he had been experiencing ceased. His heart-rate returned to normal for the first time in weeks and the pain about his heart disappeared. Praise God, he was back to normal! He vowed never to go near this kind of ministry again.

In the following weeks he often had the nagging thought that he really ought to help Janine, but the prospect of a repeat performance persuaded him that he could leave her alone and she would 'get over it'.

It was nearly a year later that Janine prayed in tongues over him at a healing service. He suddenly felt as he had done after praying over Lionel. The old palpitations returned. After the service, three people came up to John and said they felt the heavy presence of evil as she spoke in tongues over him.

For three days he was back in hell — no sleep, no peace. In desperation he rang a minister of great experience in the Midlands, Canon David MacInnes. David said he was just about to go to London on business. There was silence for a while.

'Correction,' he said, ' I was going to London. I will do my business on the phone. Can I come over for the morning and stay to lunch?'

'Stay to lunch?' thought John. 'You can stay for the month!'

David talked and prayed throughout the day with John. In the afternoon he said, 'I believe the Lord is saying that Janine has a demonic tongue. This came about because she was fearful when Lionel screamed during ministry. As she was a recently renewed Christian she was unaware of the dangers involved and vulnerable because of her fear. The result was that her original gift of tongues was distorted by the demonic during ministry.'

It seemed logical, but what a strange thought!

When David left, John did what he should have done a year ago: he invited Janine to come for ministry. She came the following day. His reasons for doing this were not as altruistic as they might have been. Not only did he now need help again himself, but a letter of resignation from the curate lay on his desk, stating that the reason was John's refusal to challenge the demonic activity that was running wild in the life of the church.

John invited two others as well as his wife to join him to meet with Janine. He explained how he had felt after she had prayed over him in tongues, and what an experienced minister had discerned: that her gift of tongues had been contaminated with the demonic when John incautiously allowed her to place her hands on Lionel during what was, in effect, deliverance ministry undertaken with no preparation and with no one supporting the ministry in prayer.

Her expression suddenly changed into a vicious hateful glare, and she pointed at John and shouted, 'You are right, and the words are . . .'

As she broke into the demonic tongue, he felt as though he was being showered with blows in a boxing ring. He blurted out the command, in the name of the Lord, that this demonic presence should be bound and go to be dealt with by Christ. He then commanded that her tongue be cleansed and made holy.

This began her healing, which took two further demanding sessions in church. Today, thank God, both she and John are free from the evil effects which resulted from that ministry and stronger for the experience. But the thought still fills John's mind: 'If only I had done something sooner . . .'

This was John's first piece of conclusive evidence that the strange and destructive feelings he had experienced were not psychological effects of trauma in childhood or later years, nor were they eruptions from the unconscious, but were very specifically the result of ministry to a person who had opened himself deliberately to the demonic. The cause and the effect were clear.

John learned the hard way, over the next few years, that coming out of a satanic group is more difficult than coming off hard drugs. It takes years rather than weeks or months, and involves many false starts and several fearful half-attempts to begin on the road to severing contact with such a group. Lionel's mind was confused beyond the wildest imagining. Black was white and good was evil. He would see the truth and the real world for a period, but would then lapse into the delusions of the satanic world. Not surprisingly he returned to the group from time to time and there, it seems, he pretended to be a 'double agent'. It was usually obvious, in retrospect, when he returned to the group. The level of chaos and disruption in the church and in personal lives went up by leaps and bounds.

On one of these returns, he later admitted, he had been the instigator of a black mass against John and the Bishop's Officer for the Ministry of Deliverance.

'Why,' John asked, 'did you do such a thing after we tried so hard to help you?'

'I wanted to prove that Christ is stronger than Satan,' he replied. It was the same old confusion and attempt at deception.

'Well, now that, without a shadow of a doubt, you know the answer, are you going to actually turn to Christ?'

John asked. Not surprisingly, Lionel changed the subject.

Later, the Diocesan Officer and John looked back to the time when Lionel had admitted initiating and taking part in the black mass. As they compared experiences, they came to realise that that time had for both of them been very dark and difficult. Life felt oppressive, and everything was hard work. Nothing ran smoothly. They described the experience as being like 'walking through porridge', with depression and despair not far away. It was all rather weird because the feelings had no logical foundation in reality. There were no obvious disasters upon which the feelings could have been based. In fact, on the contrary, both of their churches were growing and showing plenty of signs of vitality and enthusiasm.

Once again there was a clear link between cause and effect: the curses had been put upon them at the very time when they experienced spiritual desolation and emotional depression. Now they had valuable evidence of what it felt like to be under a particularly vicious curse, which was graciously robbed of its successful conclusion by the Lord. A distressing experience had become a vital insight. They were now able to see that some of the other dark times had the same distinctive marks of a curse. Far from being dispiriting, this was an exciting discovery. They began to ask themselves: 'How often, when worship seems lifeless and our spiritual lives feel dry, have our own weaknesses as individuals and as a church been aggravated by the process of cursing?'

John felt he was on to pure gold. Here was an insight into why some minor problems suddenly escalate into major incidents for no apparent reason. There has to be an added ingredient. Our own weaknesses, great though they are, could not be the sum total of the problem.

As in the field of medicine, the discovery of the cause is a good step in the direction of the discovery of the cure.

The ministry to Lionel, which involved dragging him into the church, provides an excellent case study on how *not* to minister to someone experiencing demonic oppression! At the time John was both irritated and fearful at finding himself caught up in a situation which demanded that he operate in a sphere of ministry in which he neither felt competent nor believed was valid. As a result, the ministry lacked conviction. In the end the Lord used it, as only he can, to teach many things and to open eyes to the reality of demonisation.

Further, it taught John the valuable lesson that it is quite inappropriate and unwise to use any form of coercion when ministering to people who have been hurt by occult involvement, however willing they may have been initially. Their active and willing co-operation is required throughout. It is often a great struggle for them to give that consent, and usually their resolve has to be reinforced with the loving encouragement and prayers of those involved in the ministry over a considerable period. It is rarely a straightforward process since most, if not all, of those seeking this form of help frequently change their minds and walk away for a while.

Yet this process of subjecting the helpers to the 'runaround' is a price worth paying, if they are to come to a free choice and willingly seek to be set free. In the end, the process of healing and freedom can only begin when they can face up to what they have actually done. Facing up to reality and 'owning' their actions, in their own time and at their own pace, are vital ingredients in the journey to freedom and peace of mind. John had learned the salutary lesson that there is no 'quick fix' in this form of ministry.

***

Peter and his wife arrived in Durham with a thump! Only four weeks previously Peter was a well paid business man living in Kenya. Now they were confronted with the reality of God's call to full time Christian ministry. (Mind you, God could hardly have chosen a more beautiful place for them to train!) It seemed that the road to Durham was long, but at last they were there.

His wife quickly found a job as a community physiotherapist, and Peter began the painful process of trying to resuscitate the 'little grey cells', to accommodate the rigours of a degree in theology at the University.

They settled in to the joys of life in the University, and established themselves in the local church of St Margaret's. The warmth of the fellowship there was remarkable, and Peter found himself among people who looked for, and saw, the power of God at work. For him this had always been normal. He was brought up in an Anglican clergy home and it was part of life that prayer would be answered and that God did actually look after them. This was not childhood fantasy but reality.

One aspect of the life of the church at Durham which particularly held his attention was the healing ministry. It was partly the excitement of the ministry, but that was not all; it was a natural attraction. It was encouraging to see God at work in people, and to see the sheer joy of someone healed by him. Their happiness in their newly found freedom from pain or disability was infectious. However, situations were rarely simple, and so great maturity was needed in this ministry. The road to wholeness frequently needed long-term prayer, love and care. There was often a great deal of pain, and adjusting to the will of God. The fact that the ministry in the church had moved in this direction was largely due to a doctor, Alistair Malcolm.

Alistair was a man who was easily misunderstood, his

public manner seemed to some to be rather detached, but to see him minister in the power and love of God to sick people was to draw near to the heart of the Father. Like a lot of people God uses greatly, he had his weaknesses, but one of his great strengths was that he knew them. Throughout his life he had suffered from diabetes. God never totally healed him of this. His great gift was that he saw clearly the value of combining his medical work as a GP with the ministry of healing and applied this to family therapy. He was an experienced practitioner of both, often using them in tandem and without apparent conflict of approach.

In the life of St Margaret's he was the leader of the prayer teams. It was Peter's privilege to spend many hours praying for people with him. He also prayed for Peter, who experienced deep healing from God as a result of his ministry. To say it was an education would be an understatement. Peter learned to listen to God and to differentiate between his own thoughts and those which came from God. He saw what happened to people and Alistair helped him to see the relevant medical and psychological factors which contributed to the healing process. It was all excellent preparation for what was to follow.

In due course, three happy years at Durham came to an end and Peter and his wife were faced with the daunting task of trying to find the right parish for Peter's first post. They ended up at Tamworth. It seemed the right place.

The process of making this decision took a number of visits. On one occasion they arrived on the day that John was having a healing service and Peter was invited to take part in praying for people. At the service John was going to announce that they were coming to the parish. At this time Peter's wife was obviously pregnant and the

baby was due three months before they arrived at
Tamworth. The service proceeded in a calm fashion,
and they were introduced to the congregation. About
halfway through the service Peter noticed that his wife
had disappeared. It was worrying, but he couldn't do
anything about it as he was helping John lead the service
at the front. Then someone came up and said that she
had suddenly felt ill and had gone to bed. This was totally
out of character for her, and indeed was the only time
she felt sick at that time of day during the whole of the
pregnancy.

When the time came for the congregation to greet
each other in the service, John and Peter greeted those
around them. Peter went up to a pair of men who seemed
out of it. Their reaction seemed strange when he greeted
them but he thought nothing more of it, and the next
day returned with his wife to Durham. John had
mentioned the fact that he was involved in the ministry
of deliverance from time to time, but Peter had not really
taken the statement seriously. But before leaving, he did
mention to John his unease about what had happened
to his wife during the service.

For the following two months everything went reasonably smoothly until about three weeks before the baby
was due, at which point Peter's wife became quite ill and
ended up in hospital. By chance, while doing other tests,
they discovered that the majority of her platelets (the
clotting agents in the blood) had disappeared, her liver
was failing, and the prognosis was not good. The baby
had to be born by emergency Caesarean section, and for
three to four days afterwards their lives hung in the
balance. It was a time of tremendous anxiety, though
they received great encouragement from a large number
of people in Durham, Tamworth and elsewhere in the
country who were praying for them. The situation was

all the more distressing because the doctors themselves were in the dark as to what was happening. (Documentary evidence has since been discovered of another eight cases with similar symptoms which have taken place over the last fifty years or so, and it is called the HELLP syndrome.)

As more and more prayer went on around the country, there was a growing consensus among those praying, independently of each other, that this had something to do with the demonic and Tamworth, and the aim was to stop Peter going to Tamworth. Prayer became focused on the demonic. Up to this point, Peter's experience of the demonic had been limited, and these comments considerably alarmed him. However, he did recall his sense of unease at the healing service and communicated this to John. John told him that they were experiencing an increasing amount of disruption which could not be explained rationally.

Peter's initial reaction to the situation was to become extremely angry with God for allowing this to happen in the first place, but he became even more so when faced with the possibility that it was of demonic origin. Where was the automatic protection that all Christians were supposed to have? Why pick on his wife and child?

One evening he was with Alistair explaining his feelings and sounding off as he shouted at God, Satan, the medical profession, and anyone else he could think of, when Alistair stepped in.

'You do realise, don't you, Peter, that the Lord saved them many times during those fifteen days?'

It was an abrupt reversal of the position. Was it true, or was it a coincidence that when people started praying in terms of warfare and rebuking the powers of darkness, that his wife and child came through? These were now the basic questions that he urgently needed to address.

About three months later they came to Tamworth, where they lived right in the centre of town. Their cottage was between the vast medieval church which towered over the house on one side, and a bank and a pub on the other. Directly opposite was the four-storey Co-op department store. They were, to say the least, on public display and the house wall was regarded as a convenient stopping point by the lads who used it at night on their way home from the pubs. After their arrival Peter had three weeks to learn the ropes, since John, the vicar, was then off on his annual jaunt with his caravan and extended family in tow.

Week one: any new job is a nightmare. Not only is the clergyman required to be ridiculous at times, he also has to look ridiculous. How many ways can you wear a stole? Peter never knew how complicated the care of altars could be. To his low church background the fuss was both illuminating, frustrating, and at times downright nonsensical.

Week two: all the family were ill for the week. They could not move, and were living off liquids. The result was that Peter did not learn very much.

Week three: passed in a daze. Peter was far too concerned with trying to sort out how to bury someone legally to pay too much attention to other things.

Week four: John removed himself from the scene on his summer holiday. The week passed calmly, and life progressed with a degree of what passes for normality in Tamworth.

Week five: Peter noticed something was going wrong. People he had spoken to with ease for two weeks were now giving him the cold shoulder. This went on for a few days; he started to get worried, and so made enquiries. The replies were illuminating, to say the least: 'There are rumours going around that you are involved in the occult!'

Wonderful! In five short weeks in the ministry he was already discredited. (The source of the rumour was eventually traced to one person and the extraordinary misunderstanding was resolved.)

In the space of twelve weeks he had experienced the possible existence of the demonic in many aspects of life. Was he being forced to come to terms with this and take it seriously? Or was it all just coincidence?

Peter knew he had to reassess his position, for to disbelieve in the existence of the demonic was becoming more illogical than to believe. His experience in Africa gave him cause for thought. His African colleagues had no such inhibitions. They were quite convinced that 'Satani' existed and operated—indeed, you would be the odd one out if you were not. Was belief in the action and power of Satan simply a function (to be highly derogatory) of a less 'civilised society'?

His experience was beginning to shout, 'No!'.

Surely, though, his academic background should have led him to believe that he was being emotional and drawing the wrong conclusions? On the contrary, theology taught him that there are many ways of dealing with truth, and to be wary of that which purports to be certain of the truth in all circumstances and thus plays at being God. Reason itself tends to do this.

The acid test is not what one intellectually purports to hold, but in how that applies itself when one seems to be faced with a string of real events that appear to have a demonic origin. Can one afford to ignore this element if one's wife and child are in a life-threatening situation for which there seems to be no known medical cause, and many in various parts of the country who are praying for them say there is demonic involvement? That is not the time for detached intellectual rationalisation, but a time for getting hold of the weapons that will allow the attack to be dealt with.

It was becoming clear that Peter was going to have to sort out his theory and practice, not only for his own benefit, but also for the welfare of his family. The situation looked as if these events were not entirely personal and of the family, but were closely connected with his ministry. He was beginning to grasp that he was now seeing the cause and the effect.

Four years on, John and Peter are aware continually of the demonic element in the pastoral work of the church. Healing for many has only come as a result of facing up to this unpopular conclusion. It has given a logical explanation and understanding of happenings in parish life that defy any other form of explanation or understanding. It has also, they believe, opened the door to considerably increased church growth.

The following chapters, therefore, will look at how we understand the demonic attack on the church, how it works, and how it can be dealt with in such a way that there is life-giving, God-given transformation which establishes God's kingdom in our present day.

2

A Phoney War?

Christians the world over would probably agree that because of Jesus' total obedience to the Father throughout his life, and by his death on the cross, Satan and all his works have been conquered. As it says in Colossians 1:13, 'For he has rescued us from the dominion of darkness and brought us into the kingdom of the Son he loves.' The difficulty is not here, but where we go from here. The interpretation of what this means in practical terms is by no means uniform, and it is to these various understandings we now turn.

Some current interpretations

The war is finished
A large proportion of the church throughout the world believes that because Satan has been roundly defeated on the cross, there is no longer any need to give much attention to 'spiritual hosts of wickedness in the heavenly places' (Eph 6:12 RSV) nor, for that matter, in the world around us. Spiritual evil has been dealt with, therefore we need only concern ourselves with human evil. Indeed, to give attention to Satan is precisely what he wants. He cannot look for love and worship such as we give to the

Father, so instead he seeks fearful attention. He wants people to believe he is not defeated after all, and so we play into his hands when we continually speak about the demonic.

The danger we are in, according to this view, is of treating the vanquished as though he were the victor. The best approach is to ignore Satan and all his works as much as possible.

Some time ago we gave a series of sermons on spiritual warfare, and after one service a well dressed young man approached us. He had recently joined the church from another part of the country.

'I do not understand,' he said, 'how you can give so much credence to the devil. Surely when Christ died on the cross he defeated Satan once and for all?'

In his question he neatly summarised this particular view of Satan and his works. It is a view that we instinctively want to support since no one in their right mind wants to spend time considering Satan. Indeed the majority of Christians naturally draw back from anything to do with the forces of evil.

The result of holding this view was seen, rather sadly, some time ago during a Sunday afternoon baptism at a church which conducts many such services in the course of the year. A teenage girl was becoming more and more distressed during the service, and eventually she could stand it no longer and ran out of church. After the service, the minister went to lock the church door. There he found the girl crouched in the doorway sobbing.

'What is the matter, my dear?' he asked with concern.

'I have been playing on a ouija board. I feel as though something is in me and now when I come into church I am absolutely terrified,' she replied.

The minister was at a loss how to cope so he said

somewhat feebly, 'You should not do such things!' and left her.

If one holds the view that Satan and all his works should be ignored as much as possible, there is little else except sympathy that one can give or do. This view has left many of us unprepared by the church's teaching to cope when situations arise that directly involve the demonic.

Yet so much has happened in recent times which makes it clear that the church has urgently to reassess its position. The views that are widely held on this subject measure up neither to what is happening around us in society today, nor to the biblical record:

> Be self-controlled and alert. Your enemy the devil prowls around like a roaring lion looking for someone to devour. Resist him, standing firm in the faith, because you know that your brothers throughout the world are undergoing the same kind of sufferings (1 Pet 5:8–9).

Why the caution to resist him if the possibility of being 'devoured' does not exist? 'Throughout the world' also suggests an extensive operation.

The seven sons of Sceva in Acts 19 found, to their cost, that the demonic powers were able to deliver some painful blows—even after the events of Good Friday, Easter Day, and Pentecost:

> Some Jews who went round driving out evil spirits tried to invoke the name of the Lord Jesus over those who were demon-possessed. They would say, 'In the name of Jesus whom Paul preaches, I command you to come out.' Seven sons of Sceva, a Jewish chief priest, were doing this. The evil spirit answered them, 'Jesus I know, and Paul I know about, but who are you?' Then the man who had the evil spirit jumped on them and overpowered them all. He gave them such a beating that they ran out of the house naked and bleeding (Acts 19: 13–16).

The inference here is that had the sons of Sceva truly submitted their lives to Jesus, and been in a loving and trusting relationship with him, they would have been able to stand in the victory of the cross, and the man would have been delivered (as happened on other occasions recorded in the Acts of the Apostles; eg Acts 16: 16–18). Because they used the names of Jesus and Paul only as magical incantations, the sons of Sceva were soundly beaten.

There is a clear belief here in the defeat of the devil and all his minions by Jesus on the cross. Yet the evil spirits were still able to deliver some painful lessons *after* the event on Calvary, to those who did not truly stand with Christ.

The fake war

Many today, including a large number of churchgoers, believe that all evil is of our own making and find talk of Satan and demons hopelessly outdated. There is no personal devil and therefore no spiritual contest. The problem, according to this view, lies in the heart of man which is the entire seat of all wickedness. Satan is simply a projection of the human mind.

According to this approach, we need a figure 'out there' to look at, in order to make sense of, come to terms with, and deal with the darker side of our own natures. It is highly convenient to have someone 'out there' to blame for the ills of our world rather than deal with the darkness in our own souls. By having a 'Satan' we let ourselves off the hook—he is to blame. Yet sadly, he does not exist and therefore the war is phoney.

Then again there are certain liberal schools of thought who also do not believe that Satan exists as such. He is a figment of our imagination. In the same way that you cannot have a personalised God who intervenes in people's lives, because that is morally wrong (why should God interact with some and not others, heal some and leave others to suffer?), so also the idea of a personalised Satan is wrong.

All of these views seem very convincing until you experience the demonic in a violent and personal way, as we did, or indeed until you meet someone who has been involved in the occult, and who expects you to help them.

There is also another mode of thought which says that all this talk about the devil and satanic cults is hogwash, not from a theological point of view, but based on assessment of the evidence. They would claim that it is all conservative evangelical hype. Where, they ask, is the evidence for satanic groups and for the demonic? Is it not all pure fantasy, dreamed up by churchgoers who feel they have no real purpose in our modern times? It is merely a means to find self-fulfilment in a world that has passed them by.

In 1991 Andrew Boyd wrote the book, *Blasphemous Rumours* (Fount: 1992) in which he investigated the incidences of satanic ritual abuse in recent times. It is a well balanced review of the evidence for the existence of ritual abuse, particularly of children, in western society. This highly disturbing survey of the current situation challenges us all, and particularly those of us in the church, to face up to what is going on around us. On page 317 Andrew Boyd says this:

> We must cease to imitate the three wise monkeys and force ourselves to turn and begin to face this material, listen to those who say they have been ritually abused, and be given the freedom and encouragement to discuss with one another what we are finding.
>
> If we are to open our minds, we need to suspend only our denial, whilst retaining our right and our imperative to question.

This is not a call to credulity. It is a call to make the determined choice to lower our shields of disbelief and make ourselves vulnerable to *listen*, consider, seek out and weigh the evidence, then, fighting the compulsion to react or retreat, decide with compassion and maturity how each of us can best make his response.

'Something is hard for you to understand . . . You'd better figure it out tomorrow, or today, or else we won't talk anymore'
(Child survivor of ritual abuse, Canada).

Although Andrew Boyd is writing specifically about satanic ritual abuse, we believe his comments quoted above apply equally to the whole issue of spiritual warfare. By this we mean:

- the church's combat against the satanic group's claim of a particular area for Satan.
- the church's combat against ritualistic curses placed upon the church and individuals by satanic groups.
- the counselling with love, prayer, personal support, and deliverance ministry of those who have been afflicted by the occult.
- the church's combat against territorial spirits.

If the objective of the satanists' activities includes the horrific reality of ritual abuse, then surely those who oppose this, in whatever way, are involved in a form of warfare. The Christian church has a major responsibility here and we too must face up to this reality. We must grapple with the challenge of what is happening around us in our society today.

Having said this, certain liberal insights and perspectives on this subject do have elements that are important to an overall understanding of the demonic. The emphasis on demythologising in our generation, and the continued questioning as to whether all this talk of

satanism is evangelical hype, should hold us hard to
reality and make us stand back and review the evidence
time and again.

The predominant danger that some liberal positions
warn against is over—personalisation. This helps us to
see that sin is endemic in our society and not just in the
lives of individuals. Deliverance must be related to the
wider field and must not be seen only in personal terms.

If it moves, exorcise it!

On the other hand there are a number in the life of the
church who see things very differently . Those at the
opposite end of the spectrum belong to what might be
described as the 'If it moves, exorcise it' brigade! From
time to time, the press have a field day when a church
holding this view finds itself in hot water, accused of
causing further hurt to a person already deeply mentally
scarred.

These are the horror stories that emerge periodically
in renewal and anti-renewal circles. They usually seem
to involve someone who ministers at maximum volume
with intrusive insensitivity. This standpoint is beautifully
caricatured in Adrian Plass's book *The Sacred Diary of
Adrian Plass* (Harper Collins: 1987, p 5):

> Our church is getting like an auction room. One blink and
> you get ministered to. Sit still and keep your eyes shining—
> that's my motto. This morning was Edwin Burlesford's
> fault. Forty-five minutes on 'sin'! A record nine-fruit-gum
> talk. Halfway through, I was just checking supplies when
> Edwin suddenly shouted 'LUST!', and made me drop the
> packet under my chair. Put my head down between my
> knees to locate it, then couldn't get up because Doreen Cook
> pressed her hands down on the back of my head. She prayed
> that 'our despairing brother would move from darkness to
> light'. I was all for that—I couldn't see a thing . . .

Nigel Wright in his book *The Fair Face of Evil* (Marshalls: 1989, p 13) quotes the case of a preacher and his friend who in 1980 tried to exorcise the 'spirit of Judas Iscariot' from a mentally unstable woman and unintentionally killed her by jumping up and down on her body. The judge at the trial acknowledged that they had acted with honourable motives.

The difficulty with this approach is not just that it is pastorally extremely dangerous, but also that it is theologically nuts. At the extreme it takes away our own responsibility and 'passes the buck' to Satan. It's not my fault - it was Satan! It is also in dire danger of making Satan more powerful than he really is, and as a result degrading God's power and authority.

Moving on: the path to understanding

Each of these views is prevalent in our churches and the difficulty is in finding a theory and a theology which helps us to see what is going on in the wide variety of situations that are thrown at us in twentieth-century Christian ministry, and which are illuminated by, and correspond to, the witness of the Bible.

A valid theory and theology of the demonic for our day is, we would claim, one of the most vital needs of the Christian community at this time. At stake here is not just the issue of how to deal with an individual who claims to have a problem with the demonic, but the whole future and expansion of the kingdom of God. In all the discussions about how we set about our task in this Decade of Evangelism, little has been said about dealing with the chaos and opposition caused by the demonic. The devil and his followers, as well as we Christians, have a vested interest in the Decade! How do we approach this, and what can be done to clear the ground for a 'clear run' at evangelism? We shall be exploring these issues in later chapters.

In order to do this we must have an understanding of what we are dealing with in theological terms as well as in practice. Our actions and our methods of approach must be illuminated by the evidence of the Bible and by the practices of the church throughout the centuries. It is highly unsafe to create a theology and practice of our own without reference to either the Bible or the history of the church.

Most theological thought in this area falls under the heading of 'systematic theology'. This concentrates on keeping a continuity of thought from one branch of theology to another. This is highly laudable from an academic point of view—logic and reason are the vital ingredients of the process. However, when manifestations of the demonic occur, they do not fall easily into the category of reason and logic! They can seem profoundly illogical when they happen, yet from our experience, in the end there is usually a clear and rational explanation, providing you accept the reality of the existence of the demonic in the first place.

Reason alone, however, will not lead us to this conclusion; only observation and the pursuing of a theory of what is happening, (which at first may seem medieval and hopelessly out of touch with twentieth-century rationalism) can lead us on.

As a result, our theological understanding of what is happening and what we are involved in may not seem to others to be as coherent as a systematic theology, but we would claim it is based on the foundation of Scripture and the church's practice in this field over the centuries.

As in scientific discovery, we construct a theory of what is happening in this ministry of spiritual warfare and modify it as practice demands. After being involved on a regular basis with such situations, the basic theory holds, but is continually amplified and modified.

This is not to denigrate the role of systematic theology. It has an important role in tearing down false connections and assumptions. There has to be a continued communication between systematic theology and the theology which is worked out 'at the coal face'. This will prevent excess as well as false and unChristian assumptions. In order to make sense of all this and to find our way through the maze of different understandings of Satan and his activities, we need first to consider what the Bible has to say.

The biblical witness.

The New Testament presents us with a picture of the world that Satan claims is his.

In Mark 1:12, Jesus is led out immediately after his baptism to be tempted by Satan. Matthew's account of this (4:8–11) assumes that Satan has dominion over the world. It is his to give—or, at least, Satan regards it as his to give!

In Mark, the first miracle is an exorcism (1:21ff). Jesus' ministry is recognised as having particular authority over the demonic and this causes problems (for example, the criticism of Jesus and his pungent reply in the Beelzebub controversy—Matthew 12:24 ff).

James Dunn in *Jesus and the Spirit* (SCM Press: 1978, p 18) states:

> Exorcisms were the one group of miracles to which D.F. Strauss, in his epochal work on the mythical nature of the miracle stories in the Gospels, attached a high degree of historical probability. And no developments in Gospel criticism since then have given any reason to question his judgment. On the contrary, *they have reinforced the essential historicity of Jesus's work as an exorcist.* (Italics ours)

The Old Testament is more ambiguous. There are only three references to Satan as such: Zechariah 3:1, where Satan is portrayed as the accuser; Job Chapters 1 and 2, where Satan is allowed to probe the faith and trust of Job; and 1 Chronicles 21:1, where Satan is seen as the enemy of Israel inciting David to take a census of Israel. The Old Testament picture largely reminds us that Satan is subject to God and indeed can be used by God.

In Luke 9:1, authority is given to the Twelve to deal with evil spirits. In Luke 10:17 we have the same authority given to the Seventy-two. In Mark's account of the commissioning of the Twelve (Mk 6:7) we again have the same authority given.

In Mark's account of the Great Commission (Mk 16:17) Jesus authorises the Eleven to drive out demons in his name. Even if Mark 16:9–20 is a later addition, based on the experience of the early church, it indicates that this was a common experience within the early church. Indeed, in AD 251 the church in Rome had fifty-two exorcists on its books, which was more than the number of presbyters! (Henry Chadwick *The Early Church* (Pelican, 1967 p 57). It is also noteworthy that this commission takes place after Jesus' resurrection. There is still need to drive out demons, even though Satan has been defeated on the cross.

Jesus gave authority to cleanse the demon-possessed to the Twelve and to the Seventy-two, and later this authority is given to the early church. In the Acts of the Apostles we see this continuation of his ministry, not only in healing the sick, but also in the healing of those tormented by evil spirits, and we are told 'all of them were healed' (see Acts 5:16).

Paul's famous passage in Ephesians 6:10-18 lists the armour God has given us to engage in the fight against 'the spiritual forces of evil in the heavenly realms' and in this 'dark world'. Paul highlights the intense reality of evil that he felt he was dealing with, or rather knew he was dealing with. We only need armour when people swing real swords, which actually dent the armour, making our head sing when the blow lands. There is no guarantee in the Bible of a phoney war. Paul warns us that it is a conflict of immense proportions and great significance:

> Put on the full armour of God so that you can take your stand against the devil's schemes. For our struggle is not against flesh and blood, but against the rulers, against the authorities, against the powers of this dark world and against the spiritual forces of evil in the heavenly realms. Therefore put on the full armour of God (Eph 6:11–13).

Christ placed considerable emphasis on this area of conflict. This points to the fact that he believed it to be a vital task in the mission of the kingdom. The struggle which the New Testament talks about has been internalised far too often and made subjective. It has become the struggle to resist too many sweets, and stop gazing at the opposite sex! Who needs armour for that? Strength from God, yes, but not armour.

The temptation open to everyone who deals with this area is to attempt to demythologise, see it as it really is through the eyes of modern man! We would claim that this is both arrogant and dangerous. It creates greater authorities than Christ himself and raises them up as other gods. Our experience and reflection has led us to believe that the world-view of Jesus in relation to the demonic fits the human state as we so often find it today. A world-view that dispenses with the possibility of demonisation leaves far too many unanswered questions and many hurting people still searching for healing. It also leads too many church leaders simply to walk away rather than tackle the pastoral problem before them.

Others have dealt with the problems brought to them in this whole area by 'skating over' the issue of the demonic. When pressed into doing something they have simply said a prayer which brings to mind Jesus' victory on the cross and made general reference to the situation they find themselves in. Since this seems to achieve little they are reinforced in the view that, in fact, there is little that can or need be done. It is a phoney war.

The root of the problem seems to be in western culture and the gods we actually live by, not the God we purport to live by. While the Enlightenment gave western culture tremendous advantages, it placed reason as the God of the Bible: anything which was not reasonable had to be jettisoned. The West is in the minority of the world population in holding this view, and we have to ask at what point do we suspend disbelief, and are open to the possibility that our world-view is flawed? We need to return to a world-view that is rooted in the Bible, not primarily in the Enlightenment.

Surely we are not advocating a return to the excesses of the middle ages with witch hunts, etc? Certainly not. But in our enthusiasm to ditch their ways of thinking and condemn their excesses have we not thrown the baby out with the bath water?

We really must take seriously the biblical world-view if we are to move in this area of spiritual warfare. Does this mean that we are forced to put aside reason? We do not think so , but it does mean that reason must be subject to the biblical revelation and world-view. This is not so unreasonable as it sounds! Oscar Cullman in his article 'The Subjection of the Invisible Powers' (quoted in *Territorial Spirits*, (Sovereign World: 1991, p 193) argues that this is an acceptable view for us to hold today. To quote the summary of the article:

Oscar Cullman here argues, with admirable tenacity and attention to details, that supernatural principalities, powers, rulers, thrones, lordships, and other angelic powers stand behind human governments. The fact that some of these powers may be demonic and hostile, Cullman insists, does not lead us to a heretical dualism . . .

What is the Christian's position today?

It is generally recognised among scholars and in Christian circles that we are passing through the 'in-between times'. The kingdom of God has both come and is coming into being, and we live in the tension of the two. This tension is reflected throughout the New Testament.

We have the victory of Christ, which is victory over 'sin, the world and the devil' and yet evil is ever present in our society and sin is a sad reality in all our lives. We cannot claim that they are powerless ,and yet we know that ultimately we have the victory, because of the victory of Christ on the cross.

While we see there is much beauty in the world and great love in many hearts and minds, we must not be lulled into a false sense of security. Yes, the Lord is the Victor and we can rest secure in this, but the environment in which we live and move is not a neutral one, it is essentially a fallen environment, it is full of contradiction—suffering and pain as well as beauty. We cannot live entirely at ease and at one with our surroundings, as the apostle Peter makes clear: 'Dear friends, I urge you as aliens and strangers in the world . . .' (1 Pet 2:11).

Paul also tells us in Romans 8:22ff that 'the whole creation has been groaning . . .'

The environment is not only fallen, but for Christians it is also hostile, and Satan claims dominion, as the temptation of Christ after his baptism shows. He has a dominion that has been broken on the cross, but is coming into brokenness as the kingdom of God is fully established. In the meantime, we are told to watch and be on our guard. The writer of the Book of Revelation graphically outlines the situation in a few pertinent words:

> Therefore rejoice, you heavens and you who dwell in them! But woe to the earth and the sea, because the devil has gone down to you! He is filled with fury, because he knows his time is short (Rev 12:12).

In this Decade of Evangelism the words of Paul need to be taken seriously if we are to see a decade that is really about evangelism:

> For our struggle is not against flesh and blood, but against the authorities, against the powers of this dark world and against the spiritual forces of evil in the heavenly realms (Eph 6:12).

How are we to view demonic attack, both as individual Christians and churches?

Demonic attack on individuals

We came into this area of warfare from painful personal experience. It was individual experience, but how do we make some kind of sense of it?

In the Bible there are two clear forms of satanic attack. In the story of Job God allows Satan to probe Job's trust in him. Job has not done anything wrong, quite the opposite, but Satan wanted to search out his weakness. The aim of the attack, in other words, was *temptation*, and Satan's objective was to get Job to lose his trust in God and renounce him. The one condition placed on Satan's attack by God is that Job should not lose his life.

In other words, it was an *external* attack that was permitted to test Job.

However, in the exorcisms of Christ we see the expulsion of the demons who are somehow *internal*. The words used in Mark 1:25 are 'Come out of him!' The word 'demonised' is used to describe the state of such people.

Jesus was tempted by the devil in the wilderness, but by no stretch of the imagination could he be regarded as 'demonised'. Indeed, in the Beelzebub controversy in Mark 3:20ff, Jesus gives powerful evidence of how this could not be. So we have two different modes of operation—both of which are subject to the authority of God.

There would be general agreement that everyone is subject to temptation, but less agreement as to its source. Yet the very real temptation of Christ in the wilderness, and the subtlety of the temptation of Adam and Eve in the Garden of Eden, points to the clear biblical standpoint that temptation is of demonic origin. The aim of the devil's temptation of Christ was to provoke sin, that is, rebellion against God, and so destroy his work and mission. We continually underestimate the terrible consequences of sin. Yet all of it is rebellion against God, and so aligns us with Satan, which of course is his primary objective.

But how do we understand the nature of demonisation, or the internalised workings of Satan and his minions within a person? The temptation of Christ, we believe, shows us something very fundamental about the nature of Satan. Sin is what he is after, rebellion against the will of the Father. The biblical witness to this is found most forthrightly in 1 John 3:

> Dear children, do not let anyone lead you astray. He who does what is right is righteous, just as he is righteous. He

who does what is sinful is of the devil, because the devil has
been sinning from the beginning. The reason the Son of
God appeared was to destroy the devil's work. No one who
is born of God will continue to sin, because God's seed
remains in him; he cannot go on sinning because he has
been born of God (1 Jn 3:7–9).

Whatever other issues are here, one thing is clear: sin is
related to Satan. The issue of whether we sin or can sin,
is equally clear in Romans 6:1–2: 'Shall we go on sinning,
so that grace may increase? By no means!'

The interrelation of sin and the demonic is clear; what
is less clear is how this operates within a believer's life.

To understand this it is illuminating to use an analogy
commonly found in the Prophets, Psalms, Job, and the
writings of Paul: that of the law court. The picture we
have in the Book of Job of Satan coming before God
and petitioning him in order to have Job is a helpful
one. Satan is continually interested in seeking out those
who are involved in the establishment of God's kingdom.
Personal sin gives him legal ground for access, as this
constitutes rebellion against God. God, in the majority of
cases, but not always, allows the petition. It may be
argued that this is unfair—but is it? By allowing sin
access, we have gone over to Satan's side in a particular
issue. God respects our free will and then can highlight
for that person the area of sin by allowing Satan
controlled access.

In this way we learn that sin is not simply 'my little
weakness that God must understand and put up with'
but that it is the very element that crucified Christ. As
the hymn puts it:

'Twas I, Lord Jesus, I it was denied thee:
I crucified thee.

It may well be that others, discerning God's action, may
have to point out this fact to the afflicted person but the

effect is the same. In the vast majority of cases that we have dealt with, the root cause has been sin. It may be a seemingly small matter, such as taking part in a ouija board session, but this act of sin can open the door to the demonic as it is an invitation to enter. The result of such an invitation does not go away like a common cold but continues until the sin is confessed, repented of, and forgiven. It may be that the access is not exploited till much later, when for example, that person is converted and is taking an active part in the life of the church. This access is internal to the person concerned and will be rooted in the sin that has been committed.

For example we have often found that people in their youth have played on the ouija board, and at the time have thought it a bit of harmless fun. Yet when they come into the life of the church, suddenly things can go badly wrong,and this has been reversed when the sin of the 'harmless bit of fun' has been dealt with.

We have to realise that the two-pronged nature of demonic attack (temptation and demonisation) is of fundamental importance, and that they require differing forms of ministry. If there is one message that we feel the church needs to hear more clearly, it is that sin gives access to Satan and therefore has to be taken very seriously if we are to see the kingdom of God established.

Having said that, though, there are grey areas which do not necessarily lend themselves to such a clear-cut analysis. For example, the healing of the boy with an evil spirit, after the Transfiguration (Mk 9:14ff), does not have a clear link with sin, although it is obviously demonisation.

Demonic attack on the church

The liberal position, while it does not throw much light on how to deal with the demonic, does have a great

strength, namely its emphasis that we should resist
becoming individualistic but rather keep our eyes on the
wider scale of operation. There is a danger in reducing
the nature of the demonic, sin, and salvation to the level
of the individual. It reduces sin to the banal, salvation
to simply gaining one's own ticket to heaven, and the
demonic to the level of a purely personal irritation.

The Bible opens with the story of the Garden of
Eden and significantly immediately places sin and its
consequences on a global scale. When we come to look
at our churches we have to get away from seeing sin as
an individual matter and see it as a collective issue.
Likewise we need to see that spiritual warfare is not just
a concern for the individual.

Sin in the church is easy to find! It takes many forms
but the most common are, probably, gossip, anger and
rebellion against the leadership.

We readily accept that such sin exists, but do we accept
the inevitable consequence that in engaging in this we
are giving permission for the demonic to run amok in
the church's life? It has been our experience that
collective sin has allowed demonic access into the very
heart and life of the church. We find this to be
particularly painful and not a little confusing at critical
times of decision-making. As a time of decision-making
draws near that involves change, we often clearly sense
what the will of God is in this issue, and then suddenly
'all merry hell' breaks out in the church. It has happened
numerous times.

We were just about to launch out in the first direct
evangelism that our church had done for many years.
It had all been carefully prayed over and planned, and
everyone was ready to go. The Saturday before it was
launched we had a leaders' meeting. We knew at the
time that we had a problem in the leadership with clashes

over authority between two leaders within the same house group. The meeting was difficult to begin with and the worship was grim, but gradually things improved, until it came for a time to wait on the Lord and see what he had to say. Suddenly there was total confusion! It was extremely unclear what the Lord was saying, but what alerted us to a demonic element was the fact that suddenly one or two people started saying that we should not launch into this form of evangelism at this present time. The meeting was stopped, the evangelism continued, and at the time of writing we are seeing a number of young couples coming to the Lord through that means of outreach. It was a deliberate attempt to deflect the church that occurred because we had division and sin in the leadership at that time, which gave permission for demonic confusion.

The sin of the individual can therefore have much wider consequences than the particular weakness of that person. But what about the wider picture: the tempting of the whole church? Churches can have any number of temptations as a whole community. Of these perhaps the most insidious to the 'successful' church is that of pride and a lack of humility. To other churches that are struggling, the temptation is to envy and criticism. These are often collective temptations, but their starting point, at which they move from temptation to sin, is often rooted in the leadership.

If sin and temptation are operational not just at an individual level but also at a church level, where does it stop? We do not believe it does. These are national problems, global problems, and at each level we believe there can be demonic influence. But this poses the question: how then does the demonic work?

How does the demonic operate?

In the gospels we see Jesus addressing the demons by their function (e.g, deaf and dumb spirit) and getting rid of them. We see this also in Acts 16:16 where the spirit is described by its function: 'a spirit by which she predicted the future'. There is also in Mark (5:1-20) the casting out by Jesus of the demons from Legion. This is of particular note because for some reason the demons wanted to stay in the area, and we read that Jesus obliged them by casting them out into pigs nearby. Legion's words are significant: 'My name is Legion, for we are many,' and yet Jesus talks about casting out an unclean spirit in the singular. It has been the experience of a number of people involved in this ministry that with someone who seems to have a number of internal demons there is often one lynchpin. Get rid of that one and you get rid of the rest of the lesser spirits. This implies some form of demonic hierarchy. Also possibly implicit here is the idea of territorial spirits, in that the demons wanted to hang around that geographical area. Perhaps their authority—their place in the hierarchy— was inextricably linked to their geographical location.

In Ephesians 6:12 we find Paul's famous list, which consists of 'principalities, powers, world rulers, spiritual hosts' (RSV). This list also points to some kind of ascending demonic order. If this is the case we would expect to see the nature of this reflected in most or all demonic activity and in sin.

Certainly with sin you can talk about a hierarchy in scale but not in consequence, because as far as God is concerned all sin is abhorrent. But you can say that stealing a sweet is at one level, a church in pride is another, an area characterised by violence yet another, and so you can continue to move up, to the sin of nations.

If this is so, it should be no surprise when those who

have had the courage to come out of satanic groups talk about a tightly controlled hierarchical system of authority, with each person fearful of the one immediately above them, and the whole system held together by fear. This reflects a similar ascending order.

In the last three or four years this has been an area of considerable controversy in the church. Books have come out—Frank Peretti's novels, *This Present Darkness* and *Piercing the Darkness*, Peter Wagner's books on warfare (to name a few)—all investigating this area. Our general conclusion is that the concept of hierarchies in the authority structures, and in the scope of the activities of the 'spiritual forces of evil' (Eph 6:12) is useful in practical terms, but the biblical evidence is rather slender.

The problems of language

There is considerable confusion of language and understanding concerning the demonic and occultic activity as it affects the church. We have already seen that Jesus, in his ministry, deals with two kinds of attack, temptation and demonisation. One is external, trying to cause sin and rebellion, and the other is internal to the person and requires expulsion. In the chapters that follow we use the following language and this is what we mean by it:

Curses: This is the main attack on the church. It is external, and can be broadly described as temptation with the aim to provoke sin, and in certain circumstances, destruction. It is the major concern of this book.

Demonisation: This is the internal state whereby a person has allowed the demonic within as a result of rebellion against God. This is parasitic on their sin. The ministry to get rid of demonisation is called deliverance. This ministry is more in-depth than dealing with a curse, but it follows the same basic rules. The majority of this book is not concerned with deliverance as such.

Demonisation is of varying degrees, from the minor to the extreme. We do not refer to the ministry involved in the lifting of curses as deliverance, since we reserve this word for ministry to those who would seem to be demonised.

Oppression: Occasionally we use this word to describe the effects of a curse, or demonic external attack, since this is what it feels like!

Strongholds: We sometimes use this word to refer to patterns of thought or behaviour involving persistent sin and rebellion against God which, in consequence, allow constant access to the demonic.

It is inevitable that there will be a degree of overlap between these areas. It is possible for example for a curse to turn into demonisation if the sins, which allowed the curse to take root in the first place, are not addressed.

3

The Attack on The Church

Back in 1982 John and his wife visited a church they had links with in Swaziland. During their stay they visited the Diocesan Retreat and Conference Centre in Mbabane. The Warden told them that a witch-doctor who practised white magic had been invited to address the Council of Churches on the subject of witchcraft on that day, and suggested this might be of interest to them. John replied that they did not have such problems in England. The Warden somewhat prophetically rejoined that they certainly must do, but had not come across it.

Somewhat chastened, John suggested to his wife that they ought to hear what the witch-doctor had to say.

They were not prepared for the events that unfolded on that day. He burst into the room and took the meeting by storm. As he stood before the gathering of ministers, priests, nuns and church leaders, dressed in the witch-doctor's traditional costume, including a lion's tail wrapped around his head and held with a large wooden pin, he wasted no time in castigating the church for stopping the execution of the 'Lizards'. These loathsome people, they learned, practise black magic and advocate the taking of young children and sacrificing them to break curses put upon unfortunate sufferers.

In considerable and gruesome detail he described how the sacrifices are carried out.

(Three such sacrifices were reported in the local papers during their five-week visit.)

'They are everywhere!' he shouted, 'And I know for a fact that some of you are Lizards!' At this point he paused to glare menacingly at the gathering. A sharp exit seemed the obvious option, but to do so would probably have been seen as an admission of guilt!

With considerable care, he drew a clear distinction between his 'whiter than white' magic and the Lizards' disgusting practices. He then assured the meeting that he was equally as powerful as the Lizards. As if to prove this, he told them that if someone was cursed in this terrible way he could lift off the curse, double its power, and 'return it to sender'. At this he slammed his fist on the desk in front of him. Plainly they were intended to be impressed by this display of expertise.

That was Africa, but do such things happen here? Or does this only happen in 'less developed' cultures? We would say a categorical no! We come across curses on a regular basis.

* * *

It had been a hard few months since Christmas, rewarding and very fruitful in many ways, but we were feeling exhausted and in need of refreshment and renewal. A one-day conference was publicised in one of the centres of renewal that we often visit for this purpose. We duly booked.

The previous day we had been involved in demanding

ministry and the thought of a day at this powerhouse of the Holy Spirit grew more and more appealing. As we approached the centre our hopes for the day were soaring and our spirits light. The banter was flowing freely—it was going to be a good day!

As we entered the centre we all (as we later discovered) became aware of a deadness, a spiritual flatness in the air. More than that, there was a sense of pressure on and about our heads. We also felt ill and simply wanted to get out.

The speaker was making good and useful points but it was falling flat. As we looked around we saw little was connecting. People were shuffling about and looking at their watches. After what seemed like an eternity the coffee break arrived, and we moved into the adjoining room.

'How are you all feeling?'

'Terrible!' was the reply in chorus.

Strangely, the sensation had lifted in the room we were now in. We carried out an experiment. We walked back into the centre for two minutes and all the oppressive sensations came back. When we returned to the adjoining room, they lifted.

It was an experience with which we were already familiar in our Ministry at St Editha's. Over the last few years the church had been frequently cursed. We were fortunate to have come to the day conference together. We often ministered together and trusted each other. We were able to talk about such things without embarrassment, but what about the person who came alone, feeling battered, dejected, and unable to discuss such feelings with others? The inevitable response would have been to say, 'It's all my fault! I'm making heavy weather of this Christian work I'm involved in and today those splendid leaders were no doubt making sense to everyone else, but it all went over my head. I'm useless. I might as well throw in the towel and give up!'

This, of course, is why the curse was placed on the centre and the conference in the first place: to make sure as many as possible went home dispirited and dejected—another step along the road to handing in their resignations.

Why hadn't the leaders realised this? Why were some one hundred leaders of the churches in the region standing around doing nothing, while this worthwhile day course was being taken apart systematically by the opposition, thus wasting precious time, money, and manpower?

It seems to us that there is a destructive power at work in our midst which is either not being recognised, or is not being taken seriously by many in the church at large.

This, of course, raises the question: what is a curse?

Curses in general

Generally all that we say to one another can be upbuilding (a blessing), neutral, or negative (a curse). We often do not realise the power of words. For example, one of the most common problems we come across is that of people thinking that God is always condemning them and that they regard themselves as essentially bad. Nothing that one says convinces them otherwise. But if you look at the childhood experiences, we have often found that one parent or both has told them they are bad, from a very young age. If that is repeated enough times, with vicious hatred, the child believes it. I must be bad because Mummy and Daddy say so. The tragedy is compounded when this is applied to God, and it is only when the 'curse' is broken that such people can hear and take on board that God loves them unconditionally.

Words have a tremendous power, particularly when spoken by those who have a great influence over us, or when they are focused on our vulnerable areas. Unfortunately we who are parents often say critical things to our children. This is rarely demonic. For a curse to be demonic implies an active, vicious wish to destroy, that is ongoing, not just a fleeting event.

Behind blessing there is the tremendously powerful force of love. With curses there is the energy and power of anger and hate. Cursing and blessing in human terms come with the power of these emotions. This is not a vague power but a sharply focused energy, which can influence other people for good or bad. This is the reason we read in James 3:1–12 the dire warnings about the tongue: 'Likewise the tongue is a small part of the body, but it makes great boasts. Consider what a great forest is set on fire by a small spark' (v 5).

Language is a very powerful spiritual channel, and this is recognised across the world. In Islam, for example, the Qur'an is not the Qur'an unless it is in the language in which it was first written. You can have translations, but they are not the Qur'an.

The biblical witness

In the Bible we find that God engages in both blessing and cursing. Behind his blessing is his tremendous kindness, behind his cursing is his holy anger. Unfortunately when we engage in cursing it is usually a sinful act, and the power behind the curse is our hatred and desire to see destruction upon those we hate. When we engage in blessing or cursing we are bringing into action very powerful emotions that release spiritual energy. Both a curse and a blessing can then be empowered further by Satan or God respectively.

If this seems a trifle far-fetched, how many times have you prayed, 'Lord, fill me with your love for this person'? It requires an act of will on our behalf for that to happen, and God then empowers that act of will with his love. It is exactly the same principle with cursing and blessing.

In the Bible there are 158 references in the Old Testament to do with curses, and 298 references to do with blessing. In the New Testament there are 24 references to do with cursing and 87 to do with blessing. We are not dealing with a minor spiritual issue here!

A fundamental principle of cursing is found in Proverbs 26:2: 'Like a fluttering sparrow or a darting swallow, an undeserved curse does not come to rest.' This means that a curse that has no grounds of validity is totally ineffective. The grounds for validity in terms of a curse coming on a Christian individual or group is sin. If a person is vulnerable because of their sin in that specific curse-targeted area, and engaged in promoting the kingdom of God, God may allow the curse to take hold.

This is most clearly seen in Numbers 5:11–31, where a woman who is part of the community of Israel and accused of adultery is tested by being cursed:

> If she has defiled herself and been unfaithful to her husband, then when she is made to drink the water that brings a curse, it will go into her and cause bitter suffering; her abdomen will swell and her thigh waste away, and she will become accursed among her people (v 27).

God himself curses in specific situations—for example, in Genesis 3:14 God curses the serpent. Why? 'Because you have done this'—that is, caused Adam and Eve to sin. But it does not stop there. Adam and Eve are also cursed for the sin they have committed, Eve to pain in childbearing (v 16), Adam to painful toil (vv 17–19).

There is nothing outside the authority of God, and therefore curses are allowed by God. This raises the question of the nature of God, which is a much larger subject, and opens up numerous areas for discussion. We do not want to duck the questions, but they are open ones, and we do not pretend to know all the answers. It is an ongoing exploration. But the principle remains that God has authority over all and must therefore be in charge.

Balaam recognised this: 'How can I curse those whom God has not cursed? How can I denounce those whom God has not denounced?' (Num 23:8).

King David recognised the principle of God's sovereignty in 2 Samuel 16:5–14. He was going along the road and was cursed by Shimei in very specific and deadly terms: 'The Lord has handed the kingdom over to your son Absalom. You have come to ruin because you are a man of blood!' The reaction of one of David's followers is equally direct: 'Why should this dead dog curse my lord the king? Let me go over and cut off his head.' David replied, 'Leave him alone; let him curse, for the Lord has told him to.'

Shimmei then continued to curse David, pelting him with stones and dirt all the way to Jerusalem. The result was that they arrived 'exhausted'. The exhaustion may have been simply due to the hassle of getting there, but we have noticed that one of the most common effects of being under a curse is exhaustion, a feeling of being totally drained.

In the New Testament in Mark 11:12–13 Jesus cursed the fig tree because it had no fruit, and it promptly died. This was a prophetic sign of what was to come if no fruit was forthcoming from Israel. Significantly, this is immediately followed by the cleansing of the Temple.

The Bible is clear that curses are the opposite to

blessings. In Deuteronomy 11:26–28 this is laid out before the Israelites:

> See, I am setting before you today a blessing and a curse—
> the blessing if you obey the commands of the Lord your
> God that I am giving you today; the curse if you disobey
> the commands of the Lord your God and turn from the
> way I command you today, by following other gods which
> you have not known.

John's experience in Swaziland raises the issue of curses being returned at twice the force and it is interesting that Timothy Pain in his book *Blessing and Cursing* (Kingsway, 1987, p 19) reports on a tradition that exists in witchcraft 'that a causeless curse upon a Christian boomerangs back upon the one who made it.'

Occasionally we have come across Christians who believe they can do what the witch-doctor did—return the curse with vengeance! However attractive this may seem (and it is at times!) the biblical witness is clear: 'Bless those who persecute you; bless and do not curse' (Rom 12:14); and 'when we are cursed, we bless' (1 Cor 4:12).

Demonic cursing

Curses have their root in anger. With God it is holy anger, but there is also ungodly anger, the anger that wishes sinful personal destruction on some other person or place. This sinful anger is hatred and is at the core of demonic cursing.

We would say that a curse can be enhanced by Satan. This particularly applies if Satan or the demonic have been invoked in the placing of the curse.

A definition

Demonic cursing is the intense wishing of evil upon a person or group of people, empowered by the energy of hatred and anger focused upon the person or group. It can involve a deliberate intention to involve the demonic, through satanic ritual activity. The involvement of the demonic may, however, have been unwittingly invoked by the hatred and anger, such hatred and anger being Satan's currency.

Those who take part in satanic ritual activities seek to increase the energy used in the process of cursing by generating pain and fear in their victims as part of their cultic rituals. They wish to draw off the energy so created and use it to further empower the curses and also to enhance their sense of well-being. The demonic powers are specifically invoked to further empower the curse.

There is a major complication for those who carry out a curse by invoking the demonic powers. The demonic seeks to take the initiative and gain control. This is the experience of many who have been in occultic groups and have then sought to come out. They joined the group wanting power and to be in control, but ended up being controlled.

Audrey Harper, for example, relates in her book *Dance with the Devil* (Kingsway: 1990) how after a break from the satanic group she gets back in touch with them and is told: 'You've been away. But we knew you'd come back. People always come back to us.'

Indeed, those who help people to come out of occultic groups often refer to the way in which those whom they seek to help frequently lapse and return to the group for a period. This seems to be due to the degree of control that is exerted over individual members. They sought power, now they themselves are under control.

Those who have been at the receiving end of a demonic curse know that it can be a distressing experience. We ourselves have noted that strangely they seem to vary in intensity. This is, in part, due to the level of our own vulnerability, which in turn is dependent on the closeness or otherwise of our walk with the Lord.

We have noticed that when a curse is particularly intense, sometimes reference to the curse as being empowered by human sacrifice has been the key to release. In the first seven months of the year in which this book was written, release was experienced five times when reference was made in prayer to human sacrifice.

Andrew Boyd (*Blasphemous Rumours*, p 122) helped us to see a possible reason for this:

> The understanding behind occultic ritual sacrifice stems from the belief that the life-force is in the blood. The death of a person or animal is believed to release energy to please or appease Satan or another entity and give power to the celebrants. Energy is also believed to be released by pain, hence the allegations of the ritual torture of animals.

He further relates the stories of three people who claim to be survivors of ritual abuse (p 321ff). These accounts are unverified, yet they each speak of human sacrifice in the three separate groups that they were involved with. Anyone who reads the large amount of literature available today describing the experiences of those who have been members of groups which engage in ritual sacrifice will be aware of the frequent reference to human as well as animal sacrifice. It therefore does not seem utterly fanciful to believe that we may be dealing with real situations when we address the issue of curses placed upon others and upon ourselves which used human ritual sacrifice as a means to empower the curse.

How does the church experience cursing?

The church experiences the cursing of:
  1. Individuals within the church

● Leaders are a major target, since if they can be thrown off course so can the whole church

- Vulnerable people within the church; for example, if a curse of anger is put on the church, those who have unresolved internal rage and bitterness will be the most likely to be attacked
- People with crucial roles in the church, such as musicians, singers, preachers, teachers . . .

2. The church building: strategic points within the building seem to be targeted. These can include:

- The entrance; by cursing the entrance all who come in and out can potentially be afflicted
- Where the worship is led
- Where the musicians and singers are located
- Where communion takes place
- Where the ministry of healing takes place

Other forms of attack

While the major attack on the church takes the form of cursing, there are other ways which do not fall quite so easily into this category.

Church infiltration

Church infiltration by satanists is one of the commissions that can be given to an individual member. The aim is to cause disruption and ultimately the destruction of the church.

It would seem that they only infiltrate the churches whose worship and activity is sufficiently godly to disrupt—perhaps unknowingly—the activities of a local satanic group.

The method of attack is varied. For example, in our experience, it is quite common for the one preaching to be attacked by demonic curses in order to cause confusion, vagueness, and headaches. The intention is to stop the word of God being preached effectively and to prevent those hearing from understanding.

Leaders particularly are targets. The satanist will identify the weak areas in each leader, and will attempt to manipulate them, by calling on demons, and by starting gossip. The aim will be to set leader against leader, so that the church falls into division. The satanist infiltrating will make every effort to fit in and not to stand out in any way. The effectiveness of this attack is dependent upon the sins and disobedience of the leaders.

We have seen another form of infiltration, one that is deliberate only on the part of the demonic forces, and not the person through whom they come. A person joins a church, totally unaware of their own sin and weakness. They may well have had 'low-grade' occult involvement in the past, but this is not acknowledged. They then attempt to get involved in the healing ministry and other forms of counselling, but refuse to be counselled or prayed for themselves. Those they counsel and pray for often seem fine in the short term, but in the long term may develop serious problems. Their relationship with Jesus can deteriorate, and prayer stop. Added to that, when those who have been damaged then come themselves for prayer with someone else, it is often discovered that demonisation has taken place.

This is a bit like a disease-carrier, and the person concerned is often totally unaware of what they are doing. Churches can avoid this kind of infiltration simply by having good basic ground rules, such as 'those who pray for others must know healing themselves'.

A strange paradox   When a church senses that it is being cursed it can be faced with a misleading situation. The curses search out the church's actual weaknesses and sinfulness, and these are highlighted to such an extent that the church can see itself as ineffectual. Yet the primary reason it is being cursed is because it is being obedient to Christ. It is strong in faith and threatening the kingdom of darkness. At such a time, it is faced with a paradox. It appears hopelessly compromised, sinful and weak. Yet in reality, its life and worship have a strength and integrity which is threatening satanic group activities. This is so devastating to the group that it attempts to disrupt the life of the church and so prevent it robbing their rituals of effective power. Hence, you can feel as weak as a kitten and yet, in Christ, be as strong as a lion.

Defiling by desecration

One morning in 1982–83, when John was Rector of St Chad's, Lichfield, he walked round the churchyard before going into church. A freshly dug area of ground caught his eye in a part of the churchyard which had long been closed for burials. He went over to the spot and found that the grave had been opened and filled in again during the night. He was horrified to see a skull impaled on a stake in the centre of the grave.

He then went into the church in order to find out if there had been any more damage. His attention was immediately drawn to the candles on the communion table at the east end of the church. They had been removed, broken and laid across the top of the candle-sticks. When he moved closer he was able to see the words of the Lord's Prayer reflected backwards onto the polished brass cross by means of a small mirror and the signs of the zodiac drawn in candle wax on the carpet by the table.

The disturbance of the grave indicated that this was not some prank and so he called the police. In minutes the church and churchyard were swarming with police officers. When they eventually left they took the skull away for further examination.

John certainly felt there was a strange atmosphere at the east end of the church, but he put this down to his anxieties and overactive imagination. Nevertheless, he said a short prayer over the table and the surrounding area and left.

Two days later a lady who often went to the church for quiet prayer told him that the Lord indicated to her while she was praying that the area needed cleansing properly and told her to do it. She said she had to persevere for quite some time before she felt confident that the area was cleansed.

From this, John learnt that a quick prayer of vague intent in these circumstances is quite useless. Secondly, he asked himself, if horoscopes and studying the signs of the zodiac are supposed to be such a harmless occupation, why were they thought to be so effective in desecrating churches by those who drew them?

It was nearly a month later that an embarrassed policeman arrived at the rectory door with a heavy parcel.

'Would you please bury this again, sir?' he asked, handing John the parcel. John suddenly realised he had the skull in his hands! It was however reassuring to learn that it dated from the same period as the grave and almost certainly had been removed from the grave. Mercifully, it was not an unauthorised addition!

The desecration of churches is a type of curse which seeks to claim the ground in a very direct and blasphemous way. It must not be taken lightly or brushed off. It is a statement of ownership and power, and correspondingly a statement that the Christian church is powerless. It is also perhaps more widespread than is given credence.

Vera Diamond, a psychotherapist, says this as a result of dealing with children who have been ritually abused:

> I was shocked at the number of churches that are apparently used. Most of them are in regular use for worship. Sometimes the child will be taken to something like three different churches within a twenty-mile radius. I have heard from several different people that the verger, the person who had the key to the church, was involved. Most probably what happens is that people are blackmailed into being involved in some way. (*Blasphemous Rumours*).

The tragedy is that the church is often just tidied up after something like this has occurred, or, at best, a vague prayer such as John's is said. This is not good enough if the church is to be set free from demonic influence.

Territorial spirits

Territorial spirits do have a major effect when they attack a church. The attack starts when the 'territory' is being reclaimed. This occurs when, for example, the worship of a church is becoming more godly and involves a real encounter with Jesus. The effect of the attack can be a sense of deadness, irrational fear, or anger in the church members. It is almost impossible to tell what is a curse and what is an attack by a territorial spirit. The results are often the same. Only prayer and discernment will reveal the source and so the cure.

We have noted that where the attack is rooted in an area of sin that that church has condoned, and which has been going on for a number of years, the probability is that it involves a territorial spirit. Sometimes these areas of corporate sin go back centuries, and can be related to the early history of a church or area. For example, tight-fistedness with money is a real problem in a lot of churches. Our attitudes are often wrong, and so is our practice. A number of churches can testify that, by teaching and prayer, God has enabled the people to give more freely and sacrificially. But for some churches these attitudes prove extremely difficult to overcome. If this is the case, the presence of a territorial spirit may have to be addressed. This is not a curse and has to be treated differently (see Chapter 7 below).

4

Spiritual Warfare: Defence

The purpose of cursing the church is to immobilise it, cause disruption, render it ineffective, stop it growing, send it into terminal decline, and prevent it thwarting the purposes of occult groups. Inevitably the attack is largely focused on the leaders. So much can be achieved to further these ends if the leadership can be misdirected, unnerved, or compromised. But the attack is by no means limited to the leadership.

Attack is often experienced by the church collectively during worship, study groups and prayer groups, and at times of decision-making when the members meet to discuss church matters. It is amazing how regularly people overreact at church meetings and then wonder afterwards why they were so belligerent. These occasions can, of course, be explained in terms of group dynamics—strange things happen when people interact in critical situations. But after years of seeing the perverse way in which some charming Christians react in these circumstances, one wonders whether other forces are at work to stop the right decisions being made.

Specific individuals in the church seem to be targeted, since only prayer which breaks specific curses upon these people brings relief. From time to time we have prayed for half an hour or more with some distressed church members and nothing has changed, but when we have switched tack and addressed the issue of curses put upon them they have been set free.

At one time the wife of a vicar in North Staffordshire rang John. She was very concerned about her husband. She was ringing because he had just gone to the doctor suffering, she said, from intercostal neuritis. She explained that this was muscle spasms in the chest wall, causing severe pain. She was reasonably sure that it was not heart trouble, but he had been up all night writhing in agony, and pain-killers did not seem to touch it. John agreed to pray for him and keep in touch.

The next day John rang their vicarage and was surprised to speak to the vicar himself. He sounded to be 'full of the joys of spring'.

'I thought you were supposed to be ill!', said John.

He laughed and replied, 'I feel a bit of a fraud really. I was in agony the night before last, but as I sat in the surgery the pain melted away and hasn't returned.'

It was at this point that John began to suspect that the vicar had been cursed. 'Has anyone else in the church suffered similar symptoms recently?'

'It's strange you should say that,' he said. 'Several have been complaining of headaches and the feeling of a tight band around their heads, while others have had chest pains similar to mine and have felt as though the life was being squeezed out of them.'

'What have you been doing in church life that is different from usual, or challenging?'

'Well, on Palm Sunday we are going to hold an outdoor service in the middle of one of the estates in the parish. In preparation for this some of our people went on a 'prayerwalk' round the estate, praying for the Holy Spirit to prepare the hearts and minds of the people in each of the houses so that they might be receptive to the gospel. Come to think of it, some did say they felt rather peculiar as they prayed over a house down one of the streets, and I am aware that someone lives down that street who is considerably involved in occult activity.'

It did make sense! There was a logical explanation for these weird happenings after all. They had been preparing for evangelism and, as a result, they were experiencing spiritual opposition from those who had vested interests in making sure that the gospel did not reach the hearts and minds of the people in the neighbourhood. In a word, they had been cursed.

They called together those who had been on the prayerwalk and brought before the Lord what they had been doing, and their objective of seeking the opening of many hearts to the gospel. Then they broke the curses placed upon them in the name of the Lord, specifically naming their strange experiences. The symptoms lifted, and they experienced a sense of freedom and release.

Painful though this had been, it was a valuable learning experience. They discovered in a practical way that the statement 'Christ is Victor' is not just a theological statement, but something they experienced in their lives as the effects of the curses were lifted from them, and they knew afresh the love and peace of God.

This event makes us ask why it is that faithful and deeply committed Christians should experience such painful effects. Are they not protected from such things since they have 'turned to Christ, repented of their sins, renounced evil' (Anglican Baptism Service) and received the gift of eternal life?

Protection

The experience of the church members and vicar, in preparation for Palm Sunday, poses a number of

questions. In particular, it raises the whole issue of
protection. The vicar is, without doubt, a man of
God; those involved in the prayerwalk are obviously
committed Christians, yet they got 'shot up'! Why should
this be? What does the Bible say about protection?

The biblical witness

In the Old Testament, in Genesis 17, we see the covenant
made by God with Abraham. It is 'an everlasting
covenant' (v 7) made with Abraham and all his
descendants, yet we need to note it is not an unconditional covenant. It is based on obedience (v 10). When
the people are disobedient they open themselves to
destruction.

In Exodus 32, the Israelites have made a golden calf
and the consequences of that disobedience are horrific—
3,000 people were killed (v 28). So despite the covenant
being an everlasting covenant it was not a licence to do
what you please—the rebels were punished. The only
way back was by repentance.

When we look at the New Testament, the principles
of the covenant have not changed: we have been forgiven
our sins because of Christ's death on the cross, we are
new creations, and we are not under law but under grace.
Like the covenant with Abraham, it is everlasting and
dependent only on belief in Jesus: 'For God so loved the
world that he gave his one and only Son, that whoever
believes in him shall not perish but have eternal life' (Jn
3:16).

Even so, within this new everlasting covenant, rebellion
has its consequences as it did for the children of Israel:

> If we claim to be without sin, we deceive ourselves and the
> truth is not in us. If we confess our sins, he is faithful and
> just and will forgive us our sins and purify us from all
> unrighteousness. If we claim we have not sinned, we make

him out to be a liar and his word has no place in our lives (1 Jn 1:8–10).

To be under grace, and know the loving protection of God, we need to be open and honest in our relationship with him. We have to recognise rebellion for what it is and confess it. If we fail to do so 'his word has no place in our lives', and God may well allow us to be vulnerable to curses from those who wish us harm, so that we see our sin and repent.

Now it is a fact that we are all sinners, and we will never be entirely free from sin until we reach heaven, and therefore we will be continually asking for God's forgiveness, grace and protection. Indeed that is the message of the prayer Jesus taught us:

> This is how you should pray: 'Our Father in heaven, hallowed be your name, your kingdom come, your will be done on earth as it is in heaven. Give us today our daily bread. Forgive us our debts, as we also have forgiven our debtors. And lead us not into temptation, but deliver us from the evil one' (Mt 6:9–13).

As we noted in Chapter 2, it is the view of many in the church that since Christ won the victory over Satan on the cross there is no need to concern ourselves with him and his activities. Indeed, to do so is to give a prominence to him which he does not deserve. Yet here we see in the pattern of prayer given to us by Jesus himself that we should pray to be delivered 'from the evil one'. In other words, we should pray for protection from his onslaught. The word 'debt' can also be translated as sin. The Lord's Prayer reminds us that our sins must be brought before God for forgiveness and we will be forgiven if we forgive others. We ask God not to let us be tempted, and then we ask for protection from the evil one.

How many of us use the pattern of prayer given to us in this part of the Lord's Prayer as the basis of our life? If we are honest, the answer probably is few of us. Is it then surprising that we experience demonic oppression?

However, Jesus did not give us a magic formula. Protection is not automatic. It depends, rather, on whether we are open and honest with God, and experience his love so that we repent and are forgiven.

Asking for protection is bringing to mind who is in charge of the universe, and a reminder that we are loved children of the living God.

One thing is clear to us: Christians are vulnerable to cursing. There is a pressing need for Christians to sort out their thinking on this issue in order that the church can be equipped. We need to be ready to face what is inevitably going to come upon churches that seek to take this country for Christ.

Yet it is our general experience that church leaders ignore this area, and then wonder why things are so difficult at times. Difficulties are put down to circumstances and pressures, but rarely is cursing and a demonic onslaught taken account of. What a tragedy! So much anguish could be avoided if only we would face up to this.

Over the last few years we have come to realise that the effectiveness of attack upon the church or upon individual Christians relies considerably on our own sinfulness and weaknesses. Whenever either of us has experienced the telltale symptoms of a curse we have sought ministry from the other. We have come to know each other's weak areas well and by majoring on these we have usually found the entry point of the curse quite quickly. The first step is the most painful one: to take responsibility for our own sinfulness irrespective of whether it is in our conscious mind or buried deep in the past. For it was this that allowed the attack to take root in the first place. We came to see that we must ask in what way we had moved away from God and trusted in our own strength.

As we have dealt with one another in this way (not entirely smoothly!), we have come to see an important principle in operation. The account of the fall of Adam and Eve (Gen 3: 1-7) points to the fact that we human beings have free choice as to whether we follow God's will or rebel against him. This is the vital condition for us to be able to love. If there were the slightest hint of arm-twisting, love would become unreal and so be emptied of all meaning. So God took a risk on us in order for us to know the wonder of his love, by giving us that free choice. Like Adam and Eve, when we turn our backs on God and go our own way we are in rebellion against God. As we do this we take a decision to step out from his oversight and guidance. More than that, we are walking in the steps of Satan. We are walking in rebellion instead of walking in obedience and love.

This is critical in the matter of being cursed. When we rebel we step over the boundary into enemy territory, or to put it another way, by our rebellion against God we have given *authorised access* to the powers of evil into that area of our lives which is in rebellion. For example, if a man continually seeks out pornographic literature, he has given authorised access to Satan in this area of his life and he is a 'sitting duck' for any curse which is aimed at sexual weakness.

Occult attack can be good for you!

At first sight, the suggestion that demonic attack can be good for you seems as nonsensical as the proposition 'poison is good for you'. Yet our experiences and the experiences of many others indicate that occult attack can in the end be positive.

First, demonic attack seeks out our weak points and our rejection of God's ways. If this leads us to get ourselves sorted out with God, we shall as a result walk closer with him. We will then have a greater awareness of the true state of our relationship with God. As a result, we will be in far better shape for the tests that lie ahead and which may be even more demanding!

> If you have raced with men on foot and they have worn you out, how can you compete with horses? If you stumble in safe country, how will you manage in the thickets . . . ? (Jer 12:5).

We should acknowledge that this can be an 'early warning sign' that our relationship with God is not all that it should be. This is the time for rigorous self-examination and confession, leading to a full acceptance of forgiveness and total restoration to the Father's side, for which he longs.

Secondly, it can be a 'back-handed compliment' and therefore a great encouragement. It tells us that what we are doing is unhelpful to the kingdom of darkness and, by implication, most helpful to the kingdom of God. It is good to be shown from time to time that what we are doing is promoting God's kingdom on earth, and especially if that information and encouragement comes from the opposition!

An attack also tells us that what we are doing as a church is probably causing the occult rituals to be robbed of power. We are 'receiving the treatment' in order to stop us causing havoc. It would seem that such occult attacks are intended to frighten us off and make us stop doing what we are engaged in so that the occult rituals can come to their full power potential.

Thirdly, it was interesting to hear those who returned from actual combat in the Gulf and in the Falklands saying that though warfare is not to be welcomed or invited, is does help the whole force to reach a state of readiness and efficiency which would not have been possible in any other way. Units that have been to war have matured very swiftly.

In a similar way, churches that have suffered from occult attack and who have then got up from under it in God's strength and love, and have opposed the attack, have experienced rapid maturing both as individuals and as a church. It's rather strange, but we have noticed that on several occasions after an occult attack, when all the disruption has been sorted out and we look back and see that we did try to be obedient to God, the church has been in far better shape than it was before. We have come to know ourselves and our inner motives far better and to trust each other to a greater degree. Paradoxically, the church is far more healthy as a result of such attacks!

The weak points in the church's armour

We now need to look at the particular ways in which the church's weaknesses create vulnerability to attack:

Secret sin

Authorised access to the powers of evil is often caused by church members failing to deal with secret sins or weaknesses in their lives. Satan loves hidden sinfulness. We all need to be challenged regularly to look deeply into our lives and face up to the unseemly dark recesses.

Some time ago we were both praying with a lady in a leadership position who was experiencing difficulties. On this occasion we were joined by another minister. After a short time he said he was feeling rather strange and uncomfortable and asked to be excused from this time of ministry and promptly went into the next room. We continued to pray with the leader and after a short while she was back in fine form. The minister then returned to the room and we discussed how he was feeling. He said he was feeling very ill at ease and uncomfortable in our presence. We suggested that we should pray for God's guidance and he readily agreed. We happened to be standing together in the centre of the room when we began to pray.

Suddenly he fell to the floor, writhing like a snake. The light in the room was quite bright and he made his way on his stomach to a sideboard against the wall and wriggled under it into the darkness. We gently coaxed him out and this time he crawled into the shadows behind an armchair! When we challenged him he shot to his feet with arms outstretched as if praising God, but his attitude was quite false. When we challenged this in the name of the Lord he again fell to the floor and wriggled towards the cover of the curtains across the window. He then turned on his back and started clawing at the curtains with his hands and feet.

By this time the two of us were feeling exhausted, and we were anxious that he should not be subjected to any further distress. He had on other occasions been involved in ministry to others to bring them release in somewhat similar circumstances, and so we asked him to tell us what the secret sin was that was holding him bound to the evil forces. With great difficulty, he wrote a word on the wall with his finger, and this word revealed the area of sin. He then struggled to confess to God his action which had created the open channel. Within five minutes the three of us were sitting enjoying a cup of coffee together and reflecting on what we had learnt. It was interesting that he had little, if any, recollection of his antics.

There had been secret areas in his life which were in direct conflict with God. He had therefore unwittingly created wide-open channels for use by the opposition. A no to God had become a yes to Satan. There is no neutral ground where we can safely repose in our own self-centredness and self-indulgence.

Destructive criticism

Authorised access to evil attack is often caused by backbiting in the church family itself, and by focusing on particular church members for blame or verbal abuse.

Peter took the third session of a Lent course in the spring of 1992 in one of the churches in our parish and spoke about unbelief. During the evening he asked all who were there to stand and then proceeded to pray that God the Holy Spirit would come upon the gathering in power.

When he did this all present felt very warm and close to God, except three who had cold hands and shivers. They were the three members of the newly formed music group. This had been a new venture for the church, which had up to then been almost entirely traditional in its worship. The move to non-traditional forms was not smooth and these three had been subject to considerable anger and criticism from other church members.

Peter felt that they had been cursed with condemnation, so he prayed that the curse would be broken and the effects of the condemnation be lifted off them. One lady crashed to the ground, caught her head on a wooden chair, and landed on the bare boards of the church floor. This caused not a little worry—she hit that chair hard! Afterwards, though, she said that catching the chair was like going through balsa wood, and lying on the floor was like being on a mattress.

When she got up she felt serene and calm, and all three said they felt the oppression lift from them. The following week they were particularly close to the Lord.

The coldness in the hands was an indication from God that the cursing was to do with worship, as, of course, it was their hands that played the instruments.

We need to face the uncomfortable fact that where hatred is focused upon one church member by another, this vicious mental onslaught upon the other person constitutes a curse. We then do the opposition's work for them. We are actually cursing other church members ourselves. Does this seem far-fetched? Not according to Jesus.

He had a rough ride in his own home town of Nazareth when he spoke in the synagogue there. On one occasion they even attempted to throw him off a cliff (Lk 4:29). In Mark 6:1-6 we learn that they 'took offence' at him, presumably because they saw him as a local upstart who dared to stand up and teach them. Jesus told them, 'Only in his home town, among his relatives and in his own house is a prophet without honour.' Then very significantly we learn: 'He could not do any miracle there . . .'

Jesus himself was unable fully to do the Father's will in that place because the people rejected the Father's will, by their 'lack of faith' (v 6). Jesus' ministry was restricted by the vicious hatred of the supposedly faithful.

We see this paralysing effect on his ministry not once but twice in the Gospels. The second time, it happened at Bethsaida. Fortunately for us we know Jesus' views on that town from Matthew:

Woe to you, Korazin! Woe to you, Bethsaida! If the miracles that were performed in you had been performed in Tyre and Sidon, they would have repented long ago in sackcloth and ashes. But I tell you, it will be more bearable for Tyre and Sidon on the day of judgment than for you (Mt 11:21–22).

When Jesus and his disciples came to Bethsaida some people brought a blind man and begged Jesus to touch him (Mk 8:22). Jesus took the blind man by the hand and led him outside the village. This was a most unusual thing for Jesus to do. Why did he do it? With the above condemnation of Bethsaida by Jesus in mind, we can assume that it had something to do with their wilful rebellion against God and their stubborn unbelief. We then learn a shocking fact (v 24). This was the only occasion when Jesus' ministry did not go 'according to plan', and Jesus had to put his hands on the blind man's eyes a second time. This time all was well, the man could now see everything clearly. Could it be that the unbelief, due to the town's rebellion against God and their rejection of God's sovereignty, had restricted the healing ministry of Jesus?

It is clear that the problem did not lie with Jesus. Jesus, irrespective of the situation, could carry out the Father's will. The effect of the unbelief, though, dramatically affected the person's ability to receive healing. Because Jesus respects our decisions, he will only move us as far as our faith and trust will take us, and that equally applies to healing. It is significant that Jesus' concluding words were: 'Don't go into the village.' In other words, do not return to unbelief.

We would claim that because the people no longer believe that Jesus can act in power, the church frequently resists the true work of God and unbelief cripples the church's work and mission today, just as it did on those two occasions.

It is essential for our health and well-being, and for the enlargement of the work of the church, that we recognise that we can stubbornly refuse to welcome God's activity among us in a similar way to the people of Nazareth and Bethsaida. The consequences of this particularly during this Decade of Evangelism are critical.

The accepted Christian mode of behaviour which includes smiling sweetly at each other and even hugging each other, but which permits us to assassinate each other's good name behind backs is not a harmless churchgoer's pastime. It is a deadly process of mutual cursing which inflicts untold harm on each other. It tears down the church's defences, creates authorised access for the powers of evil, and opens channels right into the heart of the church's life which satanic groups can use. The effects of this on the individual are many, but a common experience is a sense of unreality and confusion.

This seems to be endemic. Does this mean that it cannot be stemmed? We would argue no—it can be challenged effectively. When church members face the consequences of these activities, a clearer understanding develops and a greater motivation to change grows. We have tried lovingly to challenge these things whenever we hear about them, and the view is gradually gaining ground that the old ways can no longer be seen as acceptable in church circles.

Hurtful experiences

Weaknesses can be caused by the hurts others inflict upon us in life. Sexual abuse is the hurt that usually springs to mind, but there are other hurts experienced in early childhood and even in the womb which can create vulnerability. These create weaknesses which can somehow be exploited through cursing.

For example, a person who is unsure of their own father's love often finds it very difficult to trust their heavenly Father's love. This lack of trust is itself a weakness which can be exploited by the process of cursing. The fact that the Father loves and cares for us is beyond question, as Jesus said: 'If anyone loves me, he will obey my teaching. My Father will love him, and we will come to him and make our home with him' (Jn 14:23).

Many, of course, cannot come to this understanding by their own efforts. Many hours of counselling and prayer may be needed before an understanding of the heavenly Father's reliability and love is even partially accepted.

Flouting God's will

Authorised access can be created by deliberately flouting God's will. This may be in all manner of activities and life styles, and creates possible open channels. One example is what might be described as 'low-grade' occult involvement. This might take the form of a compulsion to study one's horoscope in the daily papers or national magazines. We are told it is 'only a bit of fun', yet, as a multi-million pound industry, it requires an avid following to generate that sort of revenue. We need to realise that these guides to daily living instil a view of the interaction between us and 'the powers that be' which runs contrary to that which we find in the Scriptures. In Scripture, the future is determined by our obedience or otherwise to God's will rather than by the stars or fate.

More serious forms of occult involvement include playing on ouija boards, simulation games where one acts out evil powers, having one's fortune told, etc. These are in a rather different league from that of horoscopes, and the resulting harm can be more deeply rooted. Again they are often seen as relatively harmless, yet many have found their walk with God impaired for years and years, and relief came only when they confessed involvement and received ministry.

John was taking a confirmation preparation session. One of the confirmees, called Lucy, told him that she had played twice on a ouija board at school. On the second occasion the glass behaved in a strange way. It somehow stuck to their hands when they tried to put it down. All who took part were frightened and abandoned the session.

John suggested she remain behind for some prayer after the session. Two other members of the group, who were coming spiritually alive, volunteered to join in the time of prayer.

Almost as soon as the ministry began it became obvious this was not a run of the mill confession of this activity. Lucy was struggling under a great weight which considerably frightened her, not to mention the two new Christians. Within seconds they were deep into spiritual warfare. It became clear that this was a murderous spirit, a spirit of death.

John suddenly remembered that she had attempted suicide eighteen months previously. At this point, he greatly regretted involving the new Christians, but it was too late to do anything about that now. Before release eventually came twenty minutes later, Lucy experienced frightening sensations of great weights being placed upon her. She slumped back into her seat absolutely exhausted but showing signs of a new serenity. John then prayed over her to close the open channels caused by the sin, and asked the Lord to fill her with his love and his Holy Spirit.

The next day she was in fine form, and ever since that day she has grown in maturity and closeness to God. However the two new Christians and John were experiencing considerable oppression, and each had to receive ministry to release this. It was some months later that they realised what their own weaknesses were which had made it possible for them to be oppressed in that particular way.

From this we learnt three important lessons:

- Never assume that a few sessions on a ouija board long ago will only involve routine ministry.
- Do not involve new Christians who have not been prepared for this ministry.
- Do not attempt this ministry without seeking the Lord's guidance and do not attempt it without the prayer support of other mature Christians.

To this we must add that it is essential to obtain the permission and encouragement of the leaders of the church. Satan is always seeking to persuade us to take part in this ministry in a covert way, without notifying the church leaders and without seeking their guidance in the matter. In this way we enter a state of rebellion and we ourselves have then stepped outside the God-given protection for this ministry. Havoc is then but a step away.

We have found that some of the ministry sessions with people who have played on ouija boards have been the most demanding and exhausting of all the ministry we have undertaken. So often they are not what they seem to be, and can rarely be thought of as low grade occult involvement.

Ralph lost his wife when she was quite young and for

months he was desolate. For solace he turned to the ouija board in the fond hope that he could contact her beyond the grave. After several sessions on his own at home he became hooked. After months on the board he became heavily addicted and, he later said, often started during the evening, continued through the night and well into the following day, stopping only to grab a couple of hours' sleep before he started again. By the time he met John he felt that he was totally in the control of one particularly powerful spirit.

Eventually he sought help from his local vicar and the two came to see John. Though Ralph was nervous he was entirely rational, courteous, and lucid. After a while they decided to proceed with ministry, with Ralph's agreement. John said a simple prayer committing the time to God's guidance. Ralph suddenly started speaking in an entirely different voice. 'You won't get me out!' he said.

It was difficult to resist having an argument with the voice, but they continued with the ministry. Ralph very slowly crumpled to the ground. His face contorted in agony, and all his muscles were as taut as a bow string. He took some five minutes to reach the ground. A highly skilled contortionist could not have performed the difficult movements so slowly.

The process now began in earnest. After forty-five minutes there seemed to be no further progress, but suddenly his vicar broke out in tongues in a very authoritative manner and for the first time in his life! The floodgates broke and within minutes Ralph was recovering in the side chapel, rubbing his arms and legs and wondering why they ached so much.

Immediately after this he joined the confirmation preparation group at his local church and was duly confirmed at the next confirmation. He had discovered the hard way that ouija boards are not to be recommended for harmless pastime activities or as a method to be used for communicating with the dead.

Lack of honesty among leaders

Authorised access into the centre of the church's life can be created by lack of openness and honesty among the *leaders*. Satanic groups which seek to destroy live churches are interested in the destruction of the unity, vision, and spiritual vitality of the leaders. This is not surprising since anyone seeking to gain control of a ship would seek to control the helm. If the leadership team can be made to seem confused, divided, and unsure of the direction that should be taken, then the whole body of the church becomes unnerved and demoralised. Destroy the vision of the leaders and inflame the existing sense of mistrust among them, and the church is well on the way to disaster.

We have found that in addressing these attacks it is essential that the leaders come together in an atmosphere of prayer. In this setting leaders need to look at their relationships one with another with frankness, honesty and sensitivity. This requires a high level of mutual trust within the leadership team. Ministry to each other which includes a frank admission of failings and a sensitive discussion of how we hurt each other or get on each other's nerves is vital. It is, however, difficult and painful. Leaders who only pray for others and never receive ministry themselves are dangerously vulnerable to satanic attack, since they do not know, or refuse to be open about, their own weak areas.

It is therefore crucial that churches which find themselves on the 'front line' should be vigilant in keeping an open dialogue and an atmosphere of trust among the leadership team. We found it significant that satanic groups do not trouble to infiltrate all churches, since it is only the ones they describe as 'alive' which cause them difficulty. One of the hallmarks of such churches is a strong, united, Spirit-filled leadership team which prays regularly together.

It is worth noting again the paradox that the cursing of the leadership team can be seen as an important feature in keeping them and the church 'lean and healthy'! When a curse on the leaders finds its mark and wreaks havoc among them, an 'early warning' has been given that relationships need attention, both with the Lord and with each other. Satan then finds himself unwittingly working for the health and welfare of the body of Christ.

Compromising the gospel

Authorised access is created by distorting and compromising the gospel. Recent theological critiques have, in some respects, resulted in a watering down of the orthodox Christian faith. Questions have been raised over the basic historical records; did the resurrection really happen or did it not? Where this has become part of the leaders' thinking it is very difficult to accept that God really wants to get involved with people and change lives. It is also not easy to be enthusiastic about such things as evangelism. If we have one faith among many, and there are many options why evangelise? The good news is not the Good News, it is just one message among many.

In many churches, there is a tendency to manufacture one's own gospel—take the bits you like and forget the rest. There is a danger that a church will be radically pro evangelism and renewal but ignore spiritual warfare, and this can lead the church into dangerous waters. It arises because the church becomes a target for attack and does not know it is under attack, nor how to cope with it. The issues that need addressing are ignored, people get hurt, and they suffer the consequences of a partial gospel.

Discernment—a neglected gift?

In this issue of the defence of the church the gift of discernment plays a crucial role. Yet, when people come alive in the Holy Spirit and the spiritual gifts begin to be showered on God's people, most yearn to speak in tongues, or receive the gift of healing. Sadly, some feel that the gift of discernment is the booby prize. Perhaps we should not be surprised at this because it is a most unnerving gift when first received. Yet it is a precious spiritual gift, a God-given resource 'for the common good' and is among the nine spiritual gifts listed by Paul in 1 Corinthians 12: 8–10, which are given to build up the body of Christ.

A person blessed with this gift may suddenly feel decidedly ill when approaching a particular newcomer to the church and this is quite alarming at first. We have tried to encourage church members to share this experience only with the leaders, and not to spread the word around that a particular person makes them feel ill! In this way we have often been alerted to the fact that a particular person has been dabbling in occult activity, and as they grow in the life of the church we have been able to broach the subject quite early in their spiritual journey. On other occasions it has alerted us to the possibility that a member of a satanic group is present at our worship.

If this gift of the Holy Spirit is not carefully routed through the leadership team then a 'witch hunt' could easily develop. The very last thing that one would want to see is the finger publicly pointed at an individual. The gift is for healing and wholeness and must not be used to humiliate another. To date we have found that those who have received this gift are people of sensitivity who are aware of this danger, and far from being 'tail-end Charlies' as far as the receiving of gifts is concerned, they are in the vanguard of the church's work, alerting us to the dangers of spiritual distortion due to someone's involvement in occult practices.

Discernment is a sensitive and demanding ministry which can be so easily misinterpreted by the wider church family. It is therefore essential that those so gifted have the trust and confidence of the church leadership.

5

Cleansing the Vessel: The Building

A few months after arriving at Tamworth, John led the Lent course, which was set, as in previous years, within the communion service in the ancient crypt of our medieval parish church. He introduced some of the new songs and choruses and he talked about the nature of faith and the effects of unbelief on the ministry of Jesus as well as upon the church today.

When Lent finished, several asked if they could continue meeting. John was delighted that this was the wish of the majority who attended. However, he was somewhat concerned that in terms of preparation and workload the whole year would be turned into a perpetual Lent! He suggested five 'ground rules' for the ongoing meetings:

1. There would be a mixture of hymns and songs, with the emphasis on music that gave praise to the Lord, and helped people into God's presence.
2. There would be at least twenty minutes of teaching leading to a practical application. (When Peter came he took the record with a 1 hour 10 minute talk—and no complaints.) This would be biblically based and, generally speaking, would be an exposition of the text in everyday language.

3. There would be plenty of time for the Lord to speak, and time given to waiting on him.

4. The Holy Spirit would be invited to minister to everyone present, while they stood in silence. This was often broken unintentionally as the Holy Spirit started to move deeply in people's hearts and minds, and then it occasionally became quite noisy!

5. There would be opportunity, in the time of ministry, to put into practice the aspect of the gospel that the speaker had been talking about.

Most of life's problems passed through the doors of the crypt. The majority found the Lord in stunning and unexpected ways and few claimed they were untouched by it all. It has to be said, however, that this was not a venture which met with the approval of the entire church family. It had its critics among those who did not wish to see the church change direction.

For those involved in it, they were days of wonder as well as days of disappointment. The latter was usually because a session, where a great deal of effort had gone into the preparation, fell flat for some strange reason. Despite the setbacks, the 'spiritual temperature' continued to rise. The number of people who received positive benefit from the times of ministry after the service grew, and physical healings were not at all uncommon.

When Peter came it became our practice, after these services, to review the night's events and we saw a common pattern emerging: a sense of giddiness and pains in the head, or even irrational irritation, often preceded the services where great things happened. On these occasions the symptoms lifted during the time of praise and worship. There were the other occasions, which were something of a disappointment, when the sense of oppression continued right through the evening, and the worship never got off the ground. Plainly there was opposition to the things of God. That opposition, it seemed to us, must at least in part be due to oppression of demonic origin. Some of it was of course our own fault when relationships were strained for one reason or another, or the prayer and preparation beforehand had been curtailed, but we felt there had to be more to it than that.

When we sat down to think and pray about what was happening, we realised that, being at the centre of the town, we must be a focus of opposition of many kinds. That could include a satanic group. The fact that there were members of the church itself who were very critical of the Tuesday evening service meant we were like an army in which a significant proportion of the force wanted to see the destruction and failure of some of its own objectives. It was not surprising that we experienced weakness in certain areas, and succumbed easily to what seemed like an attack from outside the church from time to time. We think it would be true to say that in several areas of its life and work the church was rapidly gaining strength as it learnt to trust the Lord more and more, but there were still these unnerving gaps.

Eventually we got into the habit of spiritually 'cleaning out' the crypt on Tuesday afternoons in preparation for the evening service and ministry time. We would stand in the crypt and seek to be open to the Lord in prayer and ask what, if anything, had been done which might disrupt the evening service. Sometimes there was little or nothing. On other occasions there seemed to be specific curses on the leaders or musicians, or general curses on the whole gathering. It was fascinating to see how the Lord clearly guided us. After we began regularly to pray over the crypt on Tuesday afternoons, the level of spiritual disruption was greatly reduced.

As the months went by we began to think that these oppressive experiences might not simply be a result of the cursing of the church, the sinfulness of individual members, or the wish on behalf of some church members that the whole Tuesday night venture would fail. There seemed to be another dimension of weakness in the church that we had not addressed. We came to see that just as individuals can be assailed by the demonic because of their own unconfessed sinfulness, so the whole building might be afflicted in a similar way. This is not to say that buildings can sin! But just as churches can be endowed with a sense of peace and holiness as a result of generations of faithful Christian prayer and witness, in the same way a church building might be affected over the centuries in a negative manner—by rebellion against God's will on the part of those who had gathered in it for whatever purpose. An added ingredient could also have been the effects of the frequent times of disaster in the life of the church and the town, when hostile forces sought to humiliate and destroy the people of Tamworth.

We looked into the history of the building and there we found plenty of pain and heartache. In the eighth century, King Offa built his royal palace and church on the site of the present church, but in 874 the Danes sacked the town and all lay in ruins until Ethelfleda, daughter of Alfred the Great, drove back the Danes in the tenth century and rebuilt the 'burh of Tamworth'. Yet again the Danes raided Tamworth in 943 and the church was destroyed. The Norman church which had replaced the Saxon church also met with disaster when in 1345 the fire of Tamworth destroyed many homes and engulfed the church. As in many other areas, the period of the Reformation and of the Commonwealth were turbulent times. The long list of names on the war memorial indicate that even in the twentieth century, great sadness and deprivation fell upon many families in the church and town.

To this we must add the many times when corruption, duplicity and unfaithfulness to the Lord afflicted the life of the church. We felt we had to repent, not only of our own sins but of those of our forebears. The building also needed cleansing of much pride. A building of such grand proportions can easily seduce those who meet there and delusions of grandeur take hold. There is an insidious pride which creeps over one during grand processions and occasions of social significance. We suffered these effects ourselves, and so it was not difficult to believe that our predecessors had suffered in a similar way.

As we began to pray over the building we noted that the spiritual atmosphere greatly improved for a while, and then the clouds seemed to roll back again, as though the effects of the ministry did not 'hold'. We began to see that this was because this ministry was like peeling an onion, removing the layers of sinfulness and pain that overlay the building. We had the feeling that when the sense of cleanliness and holiness was sustained we would have been led to the very core, and then there would be no more layers to remove. It was not until eighteen months later that we felt we had reached the point where the sinful effects of the past were not affecting the present in a negative way.

The crypt was by now too small to hold everyone. After much deliberation the church council decided in 1990 to move the parish communion with choir and organ to 9 am on Sunday mornings, and institute a family communion service at 10.45 am with music group. The depth and intensity of worship generated by this change seemed to release more of the onion for peeling. Today the building feels very different. There is a growing sense of lightness, liberation and freedom when we worship. A local group of parishes used the church for their confirmation service in the spring of 1992. Afterwards one of the vicars commented, 'This is a very holy place now.'

It was after this that we noticed that the incidences of disruption became fewer and less intense. We later learned that satanic groups drain power off churches by a 'leeching' process. In fact they have a dominion of leeching. They are able to do this, it would seem, by searching out the generational sins of a particular church (ie, the especially persistent sins which emerge generation after generation) and, by concentrating on that weakness, they leech off the energy and vitality of the church. To our delight, in the process of cleansing the church, we discovered that the sense of oppression became less sustained and less intense. Once again we were seeing that as we got down to serious business with God, the people changed, the building lost the oppressive sense of heaviness and the numbers increased.

During this exciting but often deeply disturbing period we had learnt a number of lessons:

1. The problem did not fade with the passing of time, and so the tactic of 'ignore it and it will go away' did not work.
2. There is a danger of putting all problems down to being cursed. It is human nature to seek to blame someone or something 'out there', rather than face up to our own weaknesses. We soon realised we had not discovered an easy way to solve all church problems! They were still our problems.
3. In war, soldiers on guard duty at army camps at night

often report that they thought that the enemy was near. Actually, their own fears led them to that conclusion. During the small hours of the night they began to see things that were not there. It is clearly possible to become fearful and sense some form of attack on the church, when in fact no such attack exists. Over the years we have found this problem fades, as those involved in the daily life of the church see that they have nothing to fear when Jesus is truly Lord of their lives. There is a distinction spiritually and emotionally between symptoms generated by our own fearful imaginations and those created by curses.

4. Wherever there is a challenge to the demonic there is usually the temptation to take the law into our own hands, as it were, and operate either contrary to the will of the leadership or without their knowledge. This is the road to disaster. (We look at this issue further in the next chapter.)

5. There is a danger of seeing our situation as being more seriously compromised by the demonic than it really is. Satan is a master of deception. He would love us to think that a minor denting of the defences should be regarded as a major threat requiring a 'last-ditch stand'. We need a sense of proportion in these matters. In the total ministry of the local church they need only occupy a small proportion of our time and energy. If people assume an attitude of wary unease and are continually searching for some form of attack, the central truth of Christianity has been overlooked: Jesus is unquestionably supreme, and he established that supremacy upon the cross. Our predominant attitude therefore needs to be that of Paul:

For I am convinced that neither death nor life, neither angels nor demons, neither the present nor the future, nor any powers, neither height nor depth, nor anything else in all creation, will be able to separate us from the love of God that is in Christ Jesus our Lord (Rom 8:38).

Ancient Sites

For those of us privileged to worship in a building built centuries ago and enhanced, generation by generation, with loving care, the blessings can be considerable, but there are two major problems.

First, we can fall in love with the building and put it before the Lord and his priorities for the present generation. So we fall into idolatry. This, according to the Old Testament prophets, is unfaithfulness and puts us at odds with God. Anyone who is unable to worship anywhere else other than in the beautiful local church may well have fallen into this trap. 'We love the place, O God, wherein thine honour dwells' can be a dangerous hymn if our attention is focused on the love of the building, instead of love and reverence for the Lord whose 'honour dwells' within. Satan loves idolatry since it deflects the worship from God, robs it of reality, and establishes another step along the way to drawing the worship to himself. He tried to persuade Jesus to engage in it in the wilderness, by tempting him to bow down and worship him, and rule the kingdom without having to make the ultimate sacrifice. Inevitably any form of idolatry makes us vulnerable to demonic attack should it come our way.

Secondly, the church may well have been built on an ancient pagan site. It was a deliberate strategy of our early forebears to build Christian churches and settlements on former occultic sites after consecrating the ground. While this was no doubt an admirable policy for them in their situation, it has stored up problems for our own. The repeal of the witchcraft laws about forty years ago sent signals far and wide. It said to the nation that occult activity is now considered harmless, since one assumes that the government only legislates against things that are injurious to the general public. This has opened the floodgates to such activity in our day and brought about a proliferation of groups who operate with confidence since they are no longer illegal. They now turn their attention to the former occultic sites on which many ancient churches stand and attempt to revive the old powers. Those who worship Sunday by Sunday in such a building may sense the effects of such activity.

The Revd David Woodhouse, a vicar with considerable experience in assisting those who have been involved in occult practices, states:

> They [those involved in occult rituals] would go to churches where there had been occult practices in the long-distant past and attempt to revive the old powers. There is a note for clergy here, that even though we have built churches on former occultic sites and consecrated the ground, there is a need for regular prayer and consecration of the building and the area.

Curses on the building

These are some of the common forms we and others have experienced.

Cursing of the entrances

We have often found, in prayer, curses on our door. People, when they come into the church, say to us, 'I don't know why but when I came in this morning I suddenly felt totally rejected and useless'; or it may be something else: 'I was suddenly overwhelmed by anger.' To begin with we often put this down to psychological causes, but on enquiry this did not hold water. What was going on?

It seemed that specific curses of destruction were often laid at our door, and this affected people differently. After praying and breaking the curses over the entrance the reactions stopped.

Curses involving cassettes and other objects

At a church nearby which is moving in renewal, they started to go through a difficult time. Relationships became strained and a whole host of problems arose. It did not seem, to the minister involved, that this was entirely of God! The church leaders noted that they had seen cassette tape wound round pillars in the church. They felt, after prayer, that these tapes were vehicles of curses. When they broke the curses and removed the tapes the situation improved considerably throughout the church.

Likewise we have often come across dead birds, and other rather objectionable objects placed in the church and at the door of the church. Quite what the aim of these objects is, is debatable. As far as putting on curses by a satanic group is concerned, they are a bit of an irrelevancy. Objects are not needed to put on curses. Indeed it would seem a bit strange to draw attention to a curse in this way!

So what is occurring? It would seem that there is a deliberate attempt to draw attention to the cursing of the church in order to instil fear. One of the emotions that really stops one getting in touch with God and standing in the reality of the inheritance that he has given us, is fear. If you are fearful it is very difficult to believe that you are a child of God, and a joint heir with the Son. Fear is also lack of trust in God and it would seem that it is this that allows the curse to take root, not the physical presence of the objects.

Cursing generally only takes place where a church poses a threat to the satanic group. There is no purpose in wasting resources and time on a church that does not pose a threat.

When the Lord brought us into this warfare a number of years ago, we had a very high incidence of these kinds of objects. We used to find all sorts of things. Yet recently they have tailed off. To begin with we probably reacted wrongly. We got very worked up and excited about them, and if we are truthful, a little fearful. So they achieved their purpose, which was to generate fear. Now if they happen, our response is much more measured, and certainly not fearful, which perhaps explains why they have tailed off. We are aware of the aim, so there is little point in continuing with them.

Cursing of specific places

From time to time we have become aware of curses having been placed in certain critical areas of the church. A colleague of ours was aware that there was something going wrong in a daughter-church, and so he decided along with the other ministers of the parish to go and pray in this church. The Lord led them to the altar: the altar was small, and there was a sense that the Lord was saying, 'Get right down there and deal with it.'

Now James was the smallest of the three, so it fell to him. He got down under the altar and prayed for the altar to be cleansed, and broke the curses. As he did so a foul smell arose under the altar, and then faded.

From time to time we have noticed that people come into the church and behave rather strangely. They seek to be alone and are abusive when approached in a friendly manner. When we had reports of these visits, the sense of being cursed increased and we knew we would have to deal with it. It took a while to put the pattern together, but we began to be more alert.

This pattern was again strangely at odds with what we knew about satanic cursing. It is not necessary to be physically present to put on a curse. Indeed it seems a little bizarre to draw attention to oneself in that way. The fact that curses were being put on in this way was clear, and relatively easily dealt with, as we listened to God and did what he said. The real problems came, not with the curses, but with those who had confronted the people.

Those involved took days to recover from the fear that they felt as a result of those encounters. They needed prayer and time in support and counselling. The real damage was not so much the cursing, but the fear generated. It destroyed for a while the sense of being a child of God, bringing about the need for counselling and prayer.

Cleansing the building

In dealing with these situations we have come to apply a number of principles and procedures:

1. We take serious note of any comments that the building 'is not quite right'. Those attending worship now know we will not laugh at them if they come with such unease. However it takes more than one swallow to make a summer. When two or three similar comments are made we then ask those who are given the gift of discernment to pray specifically about this. When the picture builds of some form of oppression, we organise a group to pray over the building.
2. When we feel confident that the Lord is guiding us to undertake the cleansing of the building, we arrange

for the group to meet. It often meets without us, but always with our knowledge and consent. It is helpful to have others who perhaps are unable to attend at that time to back up the activity with prayer.

We lock the church. This has proved to be essential. Often, when we left the door unlocked, the time of prayer over the building was disrupted for one reason or another by people coming in and demanding attention.

3. We then spend time in worship, and pray that we may consciously come within the sovereignty of our heavenly Father, only acting under his guidance and authority. It is good to bring to mind the true situation: this is God's world, he created it and is its true Lord and Master. Satan would love us to doubt this.

4. Now we come face to face with the great 'diluter' of this ministry—that is, praying in generalities and hedging it about with escape clauses! For example: 'O Lord, if it be your gracious will, cleanse this place, we pray . . .' – and home we go!

The time of prayer prior to the ministry established that it was the Lord's will, so the clause 'if it be your gracious will' is unnecessary. A quick waft of the hand and a general reference to the whole building rarely seems to achieve much either. There have been occasions when it seemed the right moment to verbalise the Lord's will that the whole place be restored fully to him. As that was put into words, with confidence, there was a sense of release. On other occasions, it has seemed necessary to pray over each area of the building. It is remarkable how the Lord seems to indicate whether anything untoward exists in that area, and the nature of the problem.

We have learned a great deal about our own

weaknesses as a church and about the intentions of those who wish us harm as we have done this. It is almost as though the Lord uses this time of cleansing prayer as an educational exercise. The nine gifts of the Spirit which the Lord gave to the church (1 Cor 12: 1–11) are vital in this ministry, when exercised obediently.

5. We have come to learn that particular 'awarenesses' refer to particular problems.

For example: a sudden loss of memory linked to a sense of giddiness has frequently pointed to a curse of confusion. Those who lead worship may well have found that when preparing to lead the worship, alertness and swift recollection were in short supply. We have known occasions before a service when the preacher has had trouble even remembering what the sermon was about!

On other occasions those seeking guidance from the Lord in prayer about the type of curse that has been put upon the building have suddenly felt as though a tight band has been placed around their heads. This could be linked in some way to the form of restraint used on a victim in the rituals carried out to gain power to curse the church. We have no actual evidence for this, but it is a common experience which has been noted by others as well as ourselves.

Headaches of various forms, and sensations of 'fuzziness' are common. Some find that this is a regular sign for them that all is not well and that some form of oppression is around.

Feelings of nausea seem to erupt when there is a heavy presence of evil. This could indicate that the intensity of the cursing has increased, or it may be related to experiences occurring in the group placing the curse.

Intense weariness sometimes grips those praying and

there is a feeling that all one's energy and vitality are being drained away. This is sometimes linked with a sense of despair and hopelessness. These can be signs of a curse of death, which sadly may be the result of an actual death, animal or human. Foetal sacrifice has been mentioned by some of those who have come out of satanic groups. This seems to be one of the most powerful weapons in their armoury in cursing the church.

Some symptoms can be related to a reasonably obvious curse. For example:

- feelings of irrational anger and irritation: a curse of anger.
- sudden sexual sensations: a curse of lust (possibly brought about by the sexual abuse of a victim).
- a desire to break up the proceedings: a curse of disruption.
- an irrational desire to sneer at and belittle the whole ministry: a curse of mockery.

There are of course many more, but these examples are sufficient to indicate the nature of the problem facing the church.

Major oppression which is particularly resistant can point to the fact that those cursing the church have linked groups together. The result is a considerable increase in the intensity of the curse.

Where it is felt, as a result of prayer, that a particular curse may involve human sacrifice, it is important that God's release and freedom should be extended to the person who was sacrificed. We consciously take them in prayer and place them in the arms of our loving heavenly Father. They have suffered enough. We pray for their release from the dominion of Satan and place them into God's care.

Throughout, we need to keep one question firmly in

the forefront of our minds: 'what specifically has the satanic group done in order to cause this result?' We then need to take the authority given to us by Jesus and in his name sever whichever curse has been discerned.

There is a trap for timorous Christians at this point, namely that instead of taking the authority committed to us as the servants of Christ, we retreat at the last moment, and simply pray a prayer asking the Lord to do the curse breaking for us. When this happens the curse remains intact. We have simply dodged the issue and paid the price.

Significantly, when Jesus commissioned the Twelve he gave them both the 'power and the authority' to cast out demons (Lk 9:1). Everyone involved in management in the world of commerce knows that if a person is given responsibility they must receive the express authority from above and the power to carry it out. Without this it is not possible to carry out the task and fulfil the responsibility. It is important to note that Jesus did not send out his disciples ill-equipped for the task. They were given the power to act in the name of Jesus. The Seventy-two were commissioned later in a similar manner and returned victorious: 'The Seventy-two returned with joy, and said, "Lord, even the demons submit to us in your name."' (Lk 10:17).

It is significant that they submitted in the name of Jesus and at the command of those commissioned by Jesus. If we are authorised for this ministry by the church, which is itself seeking to be obedient to Christ and acting on his behalf, there is no justification for resorting to tentative prayers rather than exercising this ministry with authority. However, it is important to note that this authority is based on our relationship with Christ. If that relationship is not there, the authority will not be there.

6. This is a very tiring ministry, and not a particularly enjoyable one, though there is immense satisfaction when the sense of freedom and peace comes to the place. The temptation is to end the ministry before the task is entirely completed. We need to face the compulsive feelings within us which prompt us to get the job done as quickly as we can and leave as soon as it is humanly possible. No one wishes to linger a moment longer than is necessary when in conflict with all that is oppressive, destructive, and evil, but none the less the last few minutes of the ministry are critical.

Time and again we have concluded the ministry without getting all present to ask the Lord if the task is complete, only to be told some time later that some went away uneasy that we had left unfinished business. Whenever that happens problems tend to recur. Granted they are usually of lesser intensity, but there is not the sense that the task has been completed. We need consciously to spend time, when we sense the main agenda has been dealt with, asking the Lord if anything remains still to be done. When we have finished there is often a sense of peace, warmth and love.

7. When we sense that this stage has been reached we break all 'after ministry' curses—that is, curses which are triggered by the breaking of the primary curse. This may seem a little over-cautious, but once again, experience brought us to this understanding. We noted that after being involved in this form of ministry, one or other of the party developed a splitting headache, or experienced giddiness and unreality. We have not had a recurrence of such symptoms since we began to deal with after-ministry curses at the conclusion of the session.

8. Following the Lord's warning (Mt 12:43–44) that

vacuums should not be left unfilled, we end the
ministry by inviting the Holy Spirit to fill the place
with his presence, power and love. We also seek to
seal vulnerable points of entry, in the Lord's name,
so that there will not be a recurrence of this particular
problem. It has to be said, however, that only when
the people of God who meet in the building cease to
live in ways contrary to the expressed will of God,
will the vulnerability really be dealt with.

Trouble in the church

On one Sunday morning the atmosphere at the worship
was particularly heavy. Some people seemed irrationally
fractious over petty issues, and generally there was a bad
atmosphere. Added to that, John was not feeling his
usual self. He experienced an ominous sense of forebod-
ing. We were puzzled as to where this all came from.
One of the people taking part in leading the worship
that day suddenly asked, 'Do you think it has anything
to do with that fire on the main altar last week?'

'What fire?' asked John. 'It's the first I've heard of it!'

'Oh, the cleaning team had to clear up burnt twigs
from the main altar cloth. Someone had set fire to them
and they've scorched the new covers,' he replied. 'They
thought it was probably done by children.'

The next day three members of St Editha's congregation were praying about life's difficulties. They became
aware of the Lord's anger and then one saw in her mind
a chalice deliberately tipped all over the main altar.
Simultaneously one of the other ladies saw red wine
running across a white linen cloth.

They then realised that this was a warning for the
church, and it could possibly point to a misuse of one of
the altars through a blasphemous act.

The awarenesses were now coming in from several

quarters: a reported fire on the main altar, a sense of oppression and fractiousness on the Sunday, and the picture of the chalice. John decided that the time had come to gather a group together after the Wednesday morning communion service to pray over the altars, and especially the one on which there had been the fire.

John took the group to the sanctuary, where they encircled the main altar. As soon as they turned to the Lord in prayer, two in the group, who had often been used in ministry and whose guidance by God has been self-evident on several occasions, suddenly became very cold—icily cold. Strangely both experienced this sensation only in the left hand and arm. On previous occasions we had sadly noted that relief from the sensation of coldness in the left arm, or the involuntary raising of the left arm as if holding a dagger, only came when the assumption was made that an act of human (often foetal) sacrifice had been carried out, and a curse from that ritual act was affecting the situation. The group then sought further guidance from the Lord.

The picture came to one of the group of a part of a foetus burnt on the altar as a blasphemous act. We needed to ask ourselves whether this was the creation of a fanciful imagination or guidance from God. There seemed a sense of 'rightness' about it which was confirmed by the rest of the group who had gathered to pray. This issue was then specifically addressed in the ministry that followed and the oppression instantly lifted and a sense of the warmth and love of God descended on the group. In prayer they placed the child into God's care and rededicated the sanctuary and altar to God.

They then moved on to the nave altar, where they experienced the same sensations and ministered in a similar way. Afterwards there was still a feeling of unfinished business and so they remained silent for a while, focusing on the Lord and his will for this ministry. Suddenly one of the group said, 'I think there is a curse of death on John.'

One of the group came against this curse. As it was broken John felt as though he had been hit in the stomach, and lurched backwards from the altar. Within minutes he felt entirely restored to the world of reality and experienced a great freedom and peace. The ministry was then concluded. The oppressive sensations lifted from the building and life returned to normal.

North Staffordshire

A church in North Staffordshire sensed that they had come under attack after they had prayed over the streets of an estate in the parish in preparation for an outdoor service. They had found several pieces of evidence that the church had been cursed, including cassette recording tape bound in particular patterns around trees and posts by the entrance to the church. They suspected that the church itself had been cursed and rang John about it. Shortly after, during May 1992, a member of the leadership team wrote to John:

Dear John,
Thank you so much for your advice last week. We in the prayer group found it most enlightening and helpful. It certainly gave us a great urge to get together as soon as possible and do some serious praying!

We met on Friday morning, in church. And as I said on the phone, we are very new at this sort of spiritual warfare, so we followed your instructions. We first became aware of the curses through the cassette tapes when you spoke at a teaching day on deliverance. We had found a tape wrapped very securely around the front pillars of the church. Our assumption was that it was kids fooling around! But we wondered at the sudden drop in attendance. After praying

around this to the best of our ability at the time, attendance
started to rise again, and the air of everything being hard
work lifted. That must have been towards the beginning of
last year. This time we found the tape the day after it must
have been put there. We suspect that it must have been
sometime during the night of Sunday 26th April. We cut
and destroyed it on Thursday 30th April, and did some
praying around the church. However, a feeling of things
not being quite right and a certain amount of not being
satisfied with what we had done persisted among two or
three of us. So we prayed again on Wednesday 6th May.
That resulted in my phone call to you. We were very much
at sea and had no idea of how to proceed. That particular
prayer group has been praying together now for four years.
They are a close group, very confident in one another, and
also very open and honest together. We trust one another
and so can get together and do things that maybe other
prayer groups here cannot. We had had a picture of an
obituary column in the local paper, and assumed that it
meant that maybe we had been cursed to death, or a death
wish had been placed on us.

When we met last Friday, it was with some trepidation.
We realised that we had to trust God completely in all of
this. We anointed one another, for protection, guidance,
and for gifts of the Spirit. We worshipped, welcomed Jesus
among us, confessed our sins, and did some more praise
and worship. Then we got down to some very serious
business with God about what was happening around
and about us. I need to say here that all of the things,
words, pictures, impressions that we received are uncon-
firmed in the sense that we have no proof. But for all that
follows, pictures and words were confirmed between one
another. So we are aware that we could be very wrong in
some, if not all that happened. But somehow I think not in
all.

We prayed to every point of the compass, as we
surrounded the altar. We chopped links between occultic
groups around us. We did everything in the name of the

Father, the Son, and the Holy Spirit, and with a chopping motion of the hand.

To the north:

We felt: the group is led by a man. They do regular sacrifice. This one had been a baby, named Amy. Abortions were involved, bodies buried under a landscaped coal-tip. There was an old influence of mine owners. A stone altar was used for the sacrifices and reminders were given about a time when we had prayerwalked in some of the area and very bad feelings were around a certain area where children play and which is open and disused. There is a brook which flows from that area all the way through this parish. It was felt that this was contaminated in some way by all the activities of the occultic group. Pictures of a dog tied to a pole, a man spinning wildly, and someone had a sudden pain in the neck and head. As we finished praying here, someone had a picture of smoke lying just above the ground, as if a battle had just finished.

To the west:

We felt: the group is led by a woman. They are the strongest. They are the ones who do the tapes and the heavy cursing. They curse marriages and health and have a great influence on many lives. It is in direct line with our front door, the entrance! It is the reason for much of the ill health that surrounds us at some times. We had a picture here of a house, cluttered, with things hanging on the wall and a cross with a jewelled centre. We also had a picture of two rats returning in that direction and their heads were cut off because they had not completed their job.

We did some very specific praying about this one. We sent burning arrows, saw balls of flame drop on certain houses, closed the sources (and heard a heavy door bang shut at this point), angels around the doorway, blood of the lamb over the entrance, hedge of thorns. We clapped hands to break the hold of this group—it felt physically very painful in our hands. We also thought that we needed to be very aware of this group and pray again. We were warned about them regrouping. Someone had a picture of reversed pins here, and a doll! Do they practise this sort of thing?

To the south:

We felt: this group is less important but is led by an ex-church leader. The curses on the vicar and his wife came mainly from this direction. They know a lot about them personally and about their family life. How? They mock the truth of the gospel and send out waves of deceit. There was a picture of a wedding ring and the feeling that somebody involved there is married to someone in our congregation. We also felt that they are badly affecting another church not far from us. Also a picture of someone being strangled by a scarf. Will our vicar be involved in this man's release? Prayed for a fear of God into the ex-church leader.

To the east:

We felt: this group is well established but not very strong compared to the others. They do curses of death on other churches and we saw other churches that have already been very badly affected. A large black cloud over one particular church, but a shaft of light broke through. The curse is now on our boundary and pushing against the first opposition that they have met. An old pottery owner's influence and monied people involved. Our finance is also cursed from here.

For all these points of the compass we prayed for definite things: breaking, bringing these activities to light, confusion returned, reflecting their own curses back, a breaking of holds, release. But we prayed for very definite proof to come to light. We prayed for the parents and baby involved in the sacrifice as you told us to. We released them and committed them to Jesus.

We then prayed inside the congregation for the showing forth of any enemy within. Prayed for cut ties, God to break through, for revelation and release. We expect to see a lot happening over the next twelve months!

I'm sorry if none of this sounds very logical or even correct. We just went with whatever we felt was right at the time. We didn't know what else to do! We all had the 'morning after the night before' feeling later. Doubts set in, the feeling of being crazy and maybe we should all be committed! But it was hard work, we all felt very worn out

If this report is of any help, good. If you think we are way off track, just let us know and we will start again. We are so aware of how little we know and how much we need to learn. We don't want to have to learn lessons the hard way if there is another way of doing it, so any help you give us is very much appreciated.

P.S. This Sunday evening service was superb! Full congregation, very good worship, and about thirty people responded and came forward to another or first infilling of the Holy Spirit. Very public ministry, very powerful, with almost everyone who was in church taking part in praying or being prayed with. A good time was had by all!

We found this letter to be encouraging. It showed us that a prayer group used to listening to God, and content to be guided by the Holy Spirit, yet applying 'sanctified commonsense' could move into this ministry and become aware of opposing occult attack. At first some of the pictures may seem a little fanciful, and discernment needs to be exercised. The information gained in this ministry is to assist in focusing the ministry as specifically as possible and to alert the church to occult attack: it cannot be used as if it were actual evidence. While we have included the letter here as a helpful example, we have disguised actual identities because such things should always remain confidential to the group and to the church leadership. All of it needs to be treated with discernment, but having done so it can build a picture of the forces ranged against the church.

The letter also showed us how easy it is to fall into the trap of returning curses to their sender. Tempting though this is we must leave that in the hands of the divine Judge. While we may call on God to confuse and rout the Enemy's servants, we are not to use their curses or repay evil with evil.

It is of interest to note that when this church took on the opposition, the worship was suddenly set free, and people responded to a call for renewing in the Holy Spirit. It is our experience that spiritually cleansing the church building has a dramatic effect on the worship, church life and the commitment of individuals to the lordship of Christ.

This is not, of course, a cure-all remedy for the ills of failing churches. If the leadership does not have its heart set on God, and if other ills are not addressed in the life of the church, there will not be any dramatic improvement in church life and attendance.

6

Cleansing the Vessel : The Individual

Cleansing inanimate objects, even churches, of a sense of oppression as a result of cursing is a less complicated procedure than attempting to release a person from such attacks. Buildings do not suffer from moral weakness, so one can concentrate on how they have been 'sinned against'. The fault lies elsewhere. When dealing with a person experiencing a sense of oppression, on the other hand, we are not dealing with an entirely passive victim. Our own failings and weaknesses must be a major part of the story. The process of discovering how a curse found its mark upon a person, and why it has been able to cause such problems, is not a simple and straightforward procedure. Yet however difficult it may be, love for the person, as well as obedience to God, prompts us to enter this arena and attempt to bring release in the name and power of Christ.

It must, of course, be a ministry which is duly authorised and which is done in a loving, sensitive and responsible manner, as we seek for the healing of the individual without further damage or hurt. It is a ministry in which the church has been involved for nearly 2,000 years, ever since Christ commissioned the Twelve and the Seventy-two to deal with demonic oppression.

First we must ask whether all the talk about the attack

on the church and about curses on individuals has any substance in reality, or whether it is all 'scare-mongering' by zealous Christians searching for a battle where none exists.

The local scene

Part of the purpose of a curse is to deal a blow without leaving evidence that it has taken place. It cannot be photographed when it takes root upon an individual and no material evidence usually exists to implicate those who carry out these attacks. Hence it is highly effective. But despite the covert nature of those who seek to curse the church, and despite the fact that their operation is in a field of activity that leaves little or no evidence, there are none the less indications that groups do exist in our own locality who engage in these activities:

1. One of the buildings adjacent to Tamworth Parish Church is the town's library and on its shelves, as in most local libraries today, is a section on witchcraft. One of the church members at St Editha's was looking through the books on the library shelves under the heading of religion, which was opposite the section on witchcraft. A group of teenagers were excitedly gathered round a book on witchcraft. When they left she went over to look at the book which had caused such excitement. As she moved closer she noticed a piece of paper in one of the other books on the same shelf. She lifted this book down and read the scribbled heading on the paper: 'Curses on the Bookshop'. Tamworth has book sections in some stores but there are no bookshops as such in the shopping centre. The only one in the town is in St Editha's Church. It seemed obvious which bookshop and staff had been the focus of their attention.

2. In the *Tamworth Herald* of Friday 22nd June 1984 the front-page story was of a police raid on an occultic group's activities in nearby woods. Arrests were made of local people who took part in the event. An eye-witness of the event stated:

It was a Friday evening in June when a call was received by the police to go to a wooded location to join others who had witnessed strange goings-on. Having met at the main road, and been informed of what had been seen, we drove in convoy along farm tracks to the edge of a wood. Being guided by the local farmer, we walked quietly along the edge of the wood to a point where we were able to enter. Very little of the night light penetrated, but we could see a camp-fire in the distance. Between ourselves and the fire the noise of chanting could be heard, and figures could be made out in the darkness.

At a signal, torches were switched on, revealing what could only be described as a number of naked bodies engaged in a 'conga' style of dance. When challenged by the light, the 'dance' stopped. All were standing lily-white in the darkness and each one to the last had a black bottom where they had been sitting on the ground.

Without embarrassment, the group were asked to return to the camp area, which they did willingly. The opportunity to dress was given and taken by all, without complaint. On asking if the group could come together around the fire, permission was given. They finished off their evening by cursing those of us who had dared to disturb this ritual! They were then conveyed away. On examination of the articles at the site, a 2 feet × 1 foot 3 inches (approximate) marble cutting-slab was found, together with a very slim, double-edged dagger about 16 inches in length. This knife was extremely sharp on both edges.

Also found was a 4 feet long, very heavy, double-edged broadsword. This had a two-handed handle with long handguard. This seemed to have some great significance,

since when the point was placed into the ground, one of
the group protested, as this action 'offended greatly'.

Also seen were various items of ritual clothing . . . One
of the party, a young woman, seemed to be very distressed
and it was found later that the reason for her attendance
was to be 'initiated' into the group. When spoken to some
time later the leader of the group confessed that as we were
approaching he felt 'the power leave us'. He could not have
known that one of those disrupting the rite was a clergyman.

After clearing the site of those assembled, and as light
began to dawn, it was seen that this was a very mature beech
wood, with a very high, thick canopy of leaves. It was also
evident that the circle was only marked by the continual use
of feet pressing the earth down into a hard surface. This
site had been used for many years, several times a year, and
after each use, the circle was covered by leaves and debris
from the ground until next time when it was uncovered
again.

No chalices or evidence of sacrifice were found, but the
'programme' for the weekend had been printed out by
computer . . .

Something important was to happen that night, for some
of the members had travelled from neighbouring counties,
and some from the south-west, a distance of some 180
miles.

Some time later the clergyman who had been at the police
raid came to see John, and asked for prayer to release
him from the oppressive sensations he had experienced
since that time. John vividly remembers that occasion.
During the ministry the clergyman said that it felt as
though a fish-hook was being pulled from his toes right
through his body to the top of his head.

He also said that it felt as though elastic was being
pulled from the left side of his head, and was resisting
letting go. Suddenly he felt entirely free of the oppressive
effects and the sense of the close presence of the Lord

was restored. He has remained free of those effects ever since.

3. A member of St Editha's was organising a social evening for the church, and so she went to a shop where she thought they might have some of the items that she needed. She later gave an account of this event:

On entering the shop I asked the gentleman behind the counter if I could pick his brains, and gave him details of why I had gone to his shop.

He asked, 'Are you Christians?' I replied with great enthusiasm that I was, thinking that I had been fortunate to find someone so quickly to help me. I continued to tell him what we wanted but I began to feel a little uncomfortable as I looked around the shop. I began to realise that all might not be what it seemed. While I was talking to the man he wouldn't look at me, he became non-committal, and stopped being helpful. I got a bit peeved with this and (I can't say why I did it) as he was thumbing through his diary I suddenly brought my hand down hard on his book to make him look at me. I asked him why he would not help us. His reply was, because we were Christians and we had caused enough trouble in the world. He still did not look at me, so I asked him why he would not look me in the eye, to which he replied, now looking at me: 'Because I have very hypnotic eyes and people are frightened of them.'

To which I replied, 'They are not hypnotic, not a bad colour, blue, but are knocking on a bit!'

At this point he said that he did not want to help us and I said, 'Why ever not?'

He replied, because he was a satanist. How could we profess to be Christians and have a picture of a man, hanging on a cross, dripping blood, for little children to look at? And how we had caused wars because of what we believed. We were selfish and out for our own ends. So I laughed at him and said that I would help him. At this moment he said, 'Will you lend me your chalice from church?'

I told him that what I had said was that I would help
him or loan him anything belonging to me, but the chalice
belonged to the church, not me. After a further conversation
about the church I left the shop.

Since being asked to write about this experience I have
had all sorts of things happen to me. A holder containing
a bouquet was literally thrown into the middle of the room,
as three of us stood and watched: the next moment the
drawer in the desk flew open on its own. A young lady
jumped up and said she was leaving because we had 'spooks'.
I went to pick the bouquet up and shut the drawer, promptly
hitting my head and bruising my forehead. We brushed this
aside as being a lot of nonsense! On going to my place of
work, on the frontage I found a dead snake . . . I have been
in mists at home that I could not explain. At one point I
thought I was going mad until I realised I needed ministry.
After this I saw that I had not kept God in the centre and
therefore had become disorientated. After realising this and
keeping him there, I was quite safe.

Neither the fact that the man claimed to be a satanist
nor that he was very interested in borrowing the chalice
from the church prove that a satanic group is in existence
in our area. But they are indications that such a group
exists.

It would seem that the man claiming to be a satanist
created a considerable level of fear in the parishioner,
as she admitted. This was largely due to the fact that, as
she herself realised, she had not 'kept God in the centre'.
The dead snake was possibly part of the campaign to
heighten fear, since fear makes it possible to lever
Christians away from their trust in God and make them
vulnerable to attack.

Sadly the success of this process is to be seen in the
strange phenomena that happened after she was asked
to write down the events that took place. The encounter
with the man claiming to be a satanist created fearful

unease and this could have created the 'energy' for the phenomena to develop.

For our present purpose we need simply to note that the encounter with the person claiming to be a satanist caused a considerable disruption in the person's life. That was all dispelled, together with the sense of living in a mist, when she addressed the issue of her relationship with God, and received ministry to release her from any oppression or curse.

4. Peter experienced his first, and never-to-be-forgotten, Christmas at Tamworth five months after his arrival. Christmas midnight communion in any town-centre church is often punctuated with several unscripted outbursts by revellers who have been attracted by the lights and the activity at the church. Tamworth is no exception. Mercifully the police 'loitered with intent' at the door on this occasion and that seemed to deter many of those coming 'just for a laugh' after imbibing at the local clubs and pubs. We felt we had overcome our crisis time when the service reached the sermon without so much as an additional murmur from the congregation. Sadly we were a little premature in our judgement!

The church was comfortably full and this meant we had to use two teams to 'communicate' (administer communion) or bless those coming to the rail. Peter communicated those on the left and John those on the right. After a while Peter came up to John and said, 'You see those two women in black over there—I suspect the Lord is saying that they are witches—what shall I do?'

John tried in vain to remember guidelines laid down for such situations in college lectures! Then he pictured the headlines in the next edition of the local paper: 'Vicar refuses Christmas communion to two distressed women. Full story on page two.'

'You'd better give them a blessing and pass on,' John said.

'I've already done that!' Peter replied.

'Then do it again!'

After a couple of minutes Peter returned. 'They're still there demanding communion,' he said.

'Then we have no choice. Give them communion,' John replied.

He watched Peter out of the corner of his eye as he returned to the first one. She received the wafer and kept it in her hand. The second received and did likewise. Suddenly, without waiting to receive the chalice, they both jumped up, turned round and swiftly made for the west end door and left the church.

Early on Boxing Day morning Peter rang John in a dreadful state. 'Can we meet in church?' he asked. When John and his wife got there, he was slumped in a chair in a side chapel and looked dreadful. 'No, it's not the 'Christmas cheer', he said. 'This all started after I blessed those two women on Christmas Eve.'

It took half an hour of prayer and ministry to discover what they had cursed him with.

We were beginning to see that curses search out our weaknesses: the weaknesses caused by the hurts of life, especially in our early years, as well as our sinfulness. Those who engage in cursing others seem to have an ability to 'plug into' the wrong assumptions we hold about ourselves, formed as a result of painful events in our childhood, in order to exploit them. This may simply be that the curses find their target where the defences are weakest, or more ominously that some of those involved in these activities study the person they intend to attack.

The wider scene

These activities are by no means confined to our locality. The church in various areas throughout the country is experiencing occult attack in differing forms. Where church buildings and churchyards are defiled, the church members can be aware of strange and oppressive sensations. The fact that such defilement takes place is illustrated by the Revd David Woodhouse. He not only seeks to help people who have been damaged through membership of satanic groups, but also counsels those who experience deep trauma as a result of being being ritually abused. This is his account of some of the activities that have taken place:

> I have worked with several counsellees who have given me permission to share their experiences regarding desecration of churches and churchyards. Some have felt a need to sit in a churchyard, usually at night, because they have been drawn there by a feeling they cannot understand. Others have been afraid to enter the local churchyard in their village or town. In counselling work they have had a memory recall of being abused or witnessing terrifying acts done to others in that place.
>
> One woman felt a compulsion on 31st October 1990 to drive to the churchyard late that evening after the end of her house group. This was not her home area where she grew up, but she realised what she was doing before leaving her car (i.e. revisiting the place where she was abused) and managed to drive to her house, quite shaken.
>
> One woman spoke to me of practices in churchyards she had been involved in as an adult member of a coven. They . . . would declare their disgust of Christianity and defile the place. They would go to churches where there had been occult practices in the long-distant past and attempt to revive the old powers . . .
>
> Other women have spoken of being made to desecrate churches when they were children in the coven. Children

and women were raped on the altar, the black mass in all
its obscenity performed, Bibles and hymn-books defiled
through urine and faeces and torn up, and chants said to
the devil. Those children were sometimes hypnotised
afterwards to think that they would contaminate churches
and Christian people ever after because of what they had
been made to do. This presents severe problems for those
recovering from satanism if they go to the church for help.
Many clergy through fear and misunderstanding reject
them as 'wicked' and this confirms the counsellee's self-
rejection.

Though not all the reports and the events that we have
outlined can be regarded as legal evidence, the sheer
number and frequency of such reports both to us locally,
and across the country, would suggest that this not a
figment of our imagination.

How do we know when we are cursed?

If we experience a sharp pain which persists, how do we
know whether it is a curse or an actual physical condition
which is creating the pain?

There are four telltale signs which indicate a curse is
in operation rather than some form of illness or physical
weakness:

1. The symptoms are unusual. It is unusual for a pain
   resulting from a curse to follow the pattern of pain
   which is due to a physical ailment.

   Headaches caused by cursing tend to be more
   stubborn and sustained than the normal run of the
   mill headache and, as with all physical pain caused
   by cursing, rarely respond to medication. Irritating
   though this is, it is one of the indications that the root
   problem is a curse, and that can be lifted far more
   quickly by prayer than medication!

Where the curse is to create a pain in the body, it does not remain located on one particular spot (as would be the case with, say, stomach-ache) but it can move around the particular region of the body in an unfamiliar manner.

2. There is no root cause in daily living. When the curse is to create an emotion such as fear or despair, the sufferer is unable to recognise any actual reason or cause for feeling fearful or depressed at that time.

3. The symptoms are, in the majority of cases, dispelled after receiving ministry. One of the very strange, but most encouraging, features of pain caused by a curse to bring irritation or distress, is the frequent disappearance of the symptoms when addressed in prayer in the name of Christ.

4. Curses on places only have effect in that location. Where a curse is put on a particular place and is intended to affect those who gather there, it is only effective while they are at that place. On leaving the location the symptoms lift. For example, a curse of confusion put on the place where the musicians play in church may give symptoms of giddiness or perhaps loss of memory, but on leaving that location the symptoms disappear.

Some time ago John experienced excruciating pains in his back, just above the kidneys. At times during that particular week he could hardly walk. It was not a pain he had experienced before. It moved from the right side to the left and back again, and then disappeared entirely, only to return two hours later. After three days he noticed that his wife kept holding the lower part of her ribs at the back. It suddenly dawned on him that she was experiencing the same problem. Sure enough, she had the same symptoms. Perhaps they had both contracted a kidney infection, they thought. When, however, they both realised that they were experiencing the same symptoms that came and went again, and that they moved around their backs, they began to be suspicious. It seemed likely that the cause was some form of curse.

They were discussing this in the kitchen, so they simply stood where they were by the sink and ministered to each other—breaking the curse in the Lord's name. The pains went instantly and have never returned.

All manner of problems can arise as a result of being cursed. These are some that we have come across:

- a sense of being utterly drained of all energy and vitality
- headaches
- a sensation of a tight band around the head
- some forms of migraine
- a pain over one eye
- a sense of coldness in the limbs
- stabbing pains about the heart
- a gripping sensation around the heart
- painful blood vessels
- weakness of the limbs
- painful lines across the body as if one had been beaten
- sense of utter depression
- irrational sense of failure
- nausea
- irrational fear
- a sense of unreality
- the loss of memory when considering crucial issues
- stumbling over the simplest of words
- irrational sense of irritation
- a feeling of being pressed in

- a sense that our relationship with God is being undermined
- feeling disorientated

We do not mean to say that if you experience any one or more of the above symptoms, you have been cursed. This needs discernment as outlined in points 1–4.

Some curses are triggered when the person in question is about to engage in an activity which would be highly detrimental to Satan's cause. John suffered his first migraine attack after taking a Sunday morning communion service and before going on to another church to preach and minister at a healing service. The symptoms were so severe he was about to ring up the vicar of the church and explain that he was unable to come. Just at that moment a parishioner arrived at the door saying he sensed God wanted him to come, though he hadn't the faintest idea why. John explained his problem and the man immediately suspected demonic disruption. He suggested a time of prayer and John readily agreed. He broke the curse of migraine in the Lord's name and forbade the enemy to frustrate the healing service. The symptoms lifted instantly. John's sight was fully restored and he drove away fifteen minutes later to go to the church where the service was to take place. The only residual effect was a very slight post-migraine headache.

This happened a second time as John was driving to the bishop's house in Lichfield. He was going to attend a meeting of those involved in the ministry of deliverance to discuss with the bishop how this ministry could be further extended. The hope was that more clergy would be licensed for this ministry. Throughout the meeting he could hardly see and his thought processes were considerably affected. The outcome of the meeting was very satisfactory and further clergy were appointed. On leaving the bishop's house, John explained his problem to one of the members of the group who is experienced in the ministry of deliverance. At that stage he was in no fit state to drive home again since his sight was considerably impaired. They stopped where they were on the pavement by the Cathedral for a time of prayer and ministry. The migraine immediately receded, John's sight was fully restored and he drove away ten minutes later, experiencing nothing more than the customary dull headache.

To date he has experienced six of these attacks. Five have been immediately prior to a vital meeting or service which would frustrate the work of Satan. The sixth was something of a mystery and was not prior to anything of strategic importance, as far as he could see. It was no doubt the exception that proves the rule!

Cleansing the individual of cursing

Before undertaking ministry to cleanse the individual of cursing, it is important to bear in mind the following principles.

First, though it may not seem so at the time, a curse can often be a 'back-handed compliment'. It frequently means that what we happen to be engaged in at that time is of great importance for the extension of God's kingdom, and a major irritation to the opposition!

Secondly, as we mentioned in Chapter 4, we must recognise a crucial but painful home-truth : a curse can only exploit and exaggerate our own weaknesses and the weakness of our relationship with God. If we succumb, *at root*, it is our own fault. Those who are strong in the Lord, confident of the intimacy of their relationship with the Lord, and sure of his limitless love for them, open and honest concerning their own weaknesses, and reliant on God's strength, will not be engulfed by a curse. It may cause minor irritation, but it will not 'get under their skin'.

When we both realised this, we became painfully aware that there was much to be dealt with in our own relationships with the Lord. We began to see that the Lord can permit curses to reach their target in order to make us aware of our weaknesses, and so to prompt us to seek a closer walk with him.

This means that a ministry to release people, rather than buildings, from the effects of a curse is a ministry that deals with the symptoms and not the disease. The root lies in the fact that we are not really doing business with the Lord. It provides temporary relief rather than a permanent solution.

Having said that, it is not always possible when someone complains of symptoms which suggest a curse, to settle down to a long in-depth session to review the person's relationship with God. Occasionally, when we have just completed a time of prayer with those about to lead worship on a Sunday morning, one of those taking part has complained of symptoms which sound suspiciously like a curse. Two minutes before taking a service is not the time for prayer and counselling! Yet something must be done straight away to relieve the symptoms if the service is to proceed.

Remedial action may be required on other occasions, because the symptoms of the curse are of such severity that the person is incapable of objective thought. That person needs to be freed sufficiently to consider the root cause of the problem. It is worth stressing again that any ministry which deals solely with the breaking of curses will only be of temporary relief. If the root cause, which must lie in the person's relationship with God (or lack

of it) is not addressed, sooner or later the person may
be back in the same state again.

Thirdly, we noted that it is in Satan's interest to
persuade those contemplating this ministry to do it in a
covert and unauthorised way. He wants to create a
situation of rebellion so that the actions which follow
come within his domain and are robbed of credibility
and of God's authority. In that way the ministry can be
distorted, robbed of power, and further hurt rather than
healing may well be the result. It is therefore essential
that this ministry is only carried out under the acknowledged authority of the church, and all necessary
consultation and authorisation is sought and given by
the leaders of the church before proceeding.

Fourthly, it would be highly inappropriate to seek to
break curses in the Lord's name where this would
increase a person's sense of fear and vulnerability. Some
people have a phobia about demonic activity which is
akin to another's fear of mice and spiders! If there is a
conviction by those with pastoral oversight that a curse
is a possible problem, prayer out of earshot can be helpful
in such situations.

There are others, who have an unwarranted sense
of their own wickedness and believe that they are
irredeemably evil. To launch into a ministry of breaking curses with them would almost certainly be most
unwise.

Then again, there are people who believe that they
are demonised to a high degree, whereas those who have
pastoral care of them are clear that this is simply not the
case. Any ministry which reinforces that view would be
most unhelpful, and even dangerous.

Where it is suspected that a curse has been placed on
a whole family including young children, or even
specifically upon a child, it would be inappropriate to

address this issue when the children are conscious that this is happening. We have occasionally prayed over children, with their parents, while they have been asleep and found this to be a helpful ministry. It has also been beneficial in reassuring anxious parents who have experienced a sense of evil oppression and are concerned for their children's welfare.

The ministry

Over the years we have developed a framework of ministry which we find helpful. It has evolved as a result of our particular outlook and situation and therefore we do not think it likely that it would be appropriate for others to use it without adaptation. The culture, church background, and theological outlook of each Christian community will have an effect on the style and content of a ministry such as we describe. Each church needs therefore to formulate a style and framework of ministry with which it is comfortable and which fits into its general approach to healing and wholeness.

Wherever possible we do not minister alone. Over the years it has become clear that several members of the church have a particular aptitude for this ministry. They are not easily intimidated, they are able to listen to the Lord in distracting circumstances and they are often gifted with the spiritual gift of the discernment of spirits. Even though ministering to break curses does not usually lead on to the much deeper and very demanding ministry of deliverance, there is always the outside possibility that that may happen. The person being prayed with may have opened themselves consciously in the past to the demonic through ouija board games and the like, and the issue of breaking a curse may turn into deliverance ministry.

We often anoint with oil those who are to take part in

this ministry in order to affirm the Lord's victory and sovereignty. The act of anointing itself brings to mind in a powerful way the supreme lordship of Christ. We are one with him in his death and resurrection when he vanquished Satan and all his works. We stand with him and we act in his name and on his behalf.

However we must stress that this is not a ministry to be led by the inexperienced or ill-prepared. Those leading the ministry need to be experienced in deliverance ministry. They ought to be people of prayer who can give time, both to the ministry and their own personal preparation. Everything depends on their relationship with the Lord, which must be such that they know the depths of his love so that no fear enters the situation. To lead such ministry fearfully is to fail to stand in the authority of Christ.

Though it is natural to feel apprehensive in such a situation, it is not right to be fearful. Time ought to be spent before the ministry discerning what God wants. For example, what opportunities exist? What pitfalls exist? Is the time appropriate for this ministry? What form should the ministry take?

In ministering to people we often ask them to stand with hands upturned, as we stand around them and as we turn to the Lord in prayer. People seem to be more open to what the Lord wants to do when in this position, rather than seated. It is much easier to hide and to be defended when seated or kneeling. It is also important for us to see their faces and to be able to speak easily with them during the ministry. We then invite the Holy Spirit to come in love and power upon the person, holding our hands over them. (When the Holy Spirit comes upon someone when no one is touching them, it is clear this is the action of our loving God, rather than some form of human intervention. Also, after John's experience described in Chapter 1, we are a little reluctant to lay on hands until we know from the Lord as well as from our own observation that there has been no demonic involvement.)

We often find that those who have been cursed (as well as those who have been involved in occult activity) experience great coldness in certain parts or over the whole of their body. Coldness in a particular area can give clues to the root of the problem (eg, cold in the left arm of the person receiving prayer—or indeed of those engaged in the ministry—can possibly point towards an act of ritual sacrifice of some form being the force which generated the curse). A sense of warmth may indicate that there is little to be concerned about. Great heat is sometimes experienced when the person is set free. A sense of nothingness seems to point to the fact that the person is either 'shut down' and not prepared to face the issues, or that the person is spiritually unaware, and this may point to other problems to face in prayer counselling later.

We realise that these experiences may be limited to our cultural setting, and may have little relevance in other settings. However, whenever the Holy Spirit is invited to come in love and power, things happen! We can all note common patterns in our own setting, and work out tentative guidelines. The danger comes when tentative guidelines become rules, and rules are set in stone. It would perhaps be convenient if we could create unchangeable rules, but each ministry session and each person brought before the Lord is unique. Textbooks do not operate in situations such as these. We can only rely on the Holy Spirit's guidance, our experience of past ministry, and an awareness that our approach is guided by biblical principles.

We became aware of the diverse nature of Christian

ministry in the whole realm of demonisation when an
African clergyman whom we respect came to England
and joined with us in a time of ministry. Suddenly he
started to blow into the person's ear, seeking to blow out
a demon. In our cultural setting that was perplexing and
misunderstood. Yet we knew him to be highly respected
in his home church and there engaged in effective prayer
counselling.

We try to enter into dialogue with the person being
prayed with, as well as with the Lord, in order to discover
what elements of the ministry, if any, are hitting the
mark. Many of us have experiences of going forward
for prayer with a particular problem, only to discover as
the prayer began that the Lord wanted to deal with
another issue. The Lord used what we were personally
aware of in order to draw us into receiving ministry to
address the deeper issues. We need to keep in touch with
how the Lord is working in the hearts and minds of those
we pray with. Otherwise they can be subjected to the
annoying situation of the Lord pressing on with the
deeper issue, while we continue to pray over them about
the original concern which brought them forward for
prayer.

There is at this point the great danger of verbal
incontinence! Many Christians have been brought up in
a tradition that seems to proclaim that if a few words
are helpful, a lot of words will be even better—especially
if we pepper the prayer with the word 'Lord' at least
twice or three times in every sentence! Far too often
those engaging in prayer for healing break into the
silence as the rest of the people engaged in the ministry
listen intently to the Lord. They do this because they are
uncomfortable with silence, or because they do not know
what to do next. This causes a certain amount of internal
anxiety which prompts them to break out into a confused

prayer which fills the gap until the ministry can be brought to an end. We have found that this ministry involves more listening that talking.

When we look at Jesus' healing ministry, it was short, crisp, and to the point. There were no long waffling prayers. We see him turning to the Father for guidance, authorisation and empowering and then he dealt swiftly with the problem. Mark's Gospel records that when Jesus healed the deaf and dumb man 'he looked up to heaven and with a deep sigh said to him, "Ephphatha!" (which means "Be opened!")' (Mk 7:34). He did not plead volubly with the Father, since, after turning to the Father and listening to him, he knew what the Father wanted. He then got on with it and did it. (Unfortuntely we often have to take more time to hear what God is saying.)

Jesus commissioned the Twelve and the Seventy-two to carry out the ministry which they saw him undertake. It is difficult to believe he trained them to operate in a manner totally different from the way which he had demonstrated. So why do those seeking to follow his guidance and undertake the Christian ministry of healing today do so in a way that is so very different from the way that he demonstrated?

This form of ministry is a *listening* ministry and when we are reasonably clear what the Lord wants done, we need to do it—simply, concisely and without dramatic additions. Some of the most effective ministry we have witnessed has been carried out with no greater volume than one would use in conversation. It was done none the less with the perceived authority of the Lord.

We have noticed that, as with severing curses on the church building, the prayer needs to be narrowly focused on the cause which the Lord reveals. Vague prayers to 'release all the curses put upon this person' are ineffectual. This seems to be partly due to the fact that the Lord uses all such occasions to reveal the real situation. If vague ministry were effective, we would not see our weaknesses, fears, selfishness and rebellion against the Lord.

Where the person coming for ministry is a woman, we have found sometimes that she experiences an irrational, overwhelming sense of guilt and betrayal which cannot be linked to any known personal situation. On rare occasions, women have had alarming pictures and sensations that correspond to those of the mother of a sacrificed child. When this has been addressed in prayer, peace and freedom return.

Release from certain curses placed upon leaders of churches has only come about when we have addressed the issue of curses which have been placed upon the leader of the church by the leader of the satanic group— a 'leader to leader' curse.

Sometimes we find that a number of curses seem to have been placed upon a person, and then a general severing of the intertwined curses seems more appropriate. On such an occasion it is not usually possible to be clear what each curse was intended to do. It is more important that attention is urgently given to the major weakness in the person's relationship with the Lord. When that is attended to, the curses seem to fall away.

When the specific curse or curses have been severed in the name of the Lord or 'in the name of the Father, the Son, and the Holy Spirit', and the person has been set free, then ministry to the 'raw nerve ends' needs to start! Tender loving care needs to be administered with prayer for the strengthening of the relationship with the Lord. It will no doubt be helpful to note the areas of weakness in the person's walk with the Lord which allowed the curses to take root in the first place. Most sessions to sever curses need further ministry to consider the primary cause of the problem—and that lies with the individual concerned and not with what a satanic group may or may not have done.

Anointing with the oil of healing is often a fitting end to the ministry and a reminder of the love and the sovereignty of God.

> You have been my refuge, a strong tower against the foe.
> I long to dwell in your tent for ever and take refuge in the shelter of your wings (Ps 61:3–4).

When the ministry is concluded, we find it helpful that those taking part in the ministry should pray with each other and, as part of that ministry to each other, sever any 'after-ministry curses'.

As with all ministry concerned with evil oppression, this ministry hinges on those receiving ministry assuming responsibility for their own situation. Unlike treatment for an ingrowing toe nail, we ourselves are the major part of the problem. When that is acknowledged and confessed, the healing process is well on the way. A curse is like a barbed fish-hook stuck in one's finger. The admission of the actual state of our relationship with God and the acknowledgement of our own weakness and sinfulness removes the barb from the hook. It only remains for it then to be gently and smoothly lifted out.

Should we minister in this way to people who are not Christians? Conversion, we believe, is the process whereby we give ourselves willingly—body, mind, heart, and spirit—to the Lord. That would suggest that the ministry we have described above would have fewer hurdles to jump where the person is a Christian. However, as we see on numerous occasions in Acts, the apostles acted with the compassion and authority of

Christ, when led to do so by him, irrespective of the faith of the person being healed. Their example should warn us against being too narrow and dogmatic, and emphasises the importance of hearing what God wants to do in any given situation.

7

Cleansing the Vessel: The Body

We live in a society that is dominated by the individual. What the individual wants is all-important. There are numerous reasons for this, but one is the historical breakdown of the extended family. The generations of the family no longer live in close proximity to each other and they meet far less frequently, if at all. This means that individuals are thrown back on their own resources. They form their own opinions with far less family involvement, and live their lives in a way that suits themselves rather than conforming with the require-ments of the extended family. In some African cultures the extended family is still the major social unit (although this is under threat from such pressures as famine and the need to move into towns to search for employment). We have both spent time in Africa and experienced the culture shock on returning to Britain. It is a salutary experience seeing British culture through the African experience. The sense of corporate activity, family bonding and community loyalty seems threadbare in England compared with the richness of African communal life.

The largest social unit in western culture tends to be the nuclear family. This is not necessarily two adults and children. A spokesperson for the marriage counselling service Relate stated on the BBC news that by the beginning of the next decade they expect the rate of marriage failure to be four out of ten marriages. It would seem that the percentage of single-parent families is rising and the family unit is getting smaller, and thus individuals are finding they have to cope on their own more and more, rather than rely on the family or wider community.

In this social situation, which affects the church as well as the rest of society, it is difficult for church leaders and members alike to see the great potential, the divinely created breadth and depth, of the corporate nature of the church. It is true that we often give lip-service to the idea of the body of Christ. We know it potentially to be of great benefit to us all and to the world in which we live, and we know it to be a concept which is theologically correct, but how rare it is for the fruit of this to reach maturity.

If it is difficult to grasp the corporate nature of the church in general, it is even more difficult to get hold of the idea of the corporate nature of sin, and the consequences of such sin in giving authorised access to the demonic. The Bible, though, often makes it quite clear how the sins of the people have a devastating effect on the whole of the community.

The biblical witness

The story of the making of the golden calf in Exodus 32 portrays Aaron as a weak leader who is persuaded by the people that there is a necessity to make a golden idol to worship. Moses takes so long in returning from the mountain that they think he has deserted them. They seek for comfort in their old ways and ask for a religious focus, a golden calf, around which they can gather for

reassurance in his absence. The one left in charge fails
to control this move towards idolatry, and bows to the
will of the people. Hence we see the flowering of sinful
idolatry which is a corporate act, permitted by the leader,
and indulged in by the people.

When God told Moses what was going on down in the
valley below, Moses pleaded with God not to bring
devastation on all the people. He was then permitted by
God to return and confront them with their sin. He
called all those who would be faithful to the Lord to join
him, and all the Levites gathered around him. Moses
then told them to kill all who remained in rebellion
against the Lord. It would seem that the rejection of the
Lord had to be dealt with if the mission of the Israelite
people was to continue.

In Leviticus 16, we again see the interrelation between
individual and corporate sin, this time as set out in the
atonement rituals. Aaron has to offer a bull for his own
sin and that of his family. Then two goats are brought—
one is to be a sin offering, the other is to be a 'scapegoat'.
The scapegoat is to have all the sins of the people
confessed over it and be sent into the desert. It is a
symbolic corporate act. The sins of all the people are
loaded onto the scapegoat and the body of the people
cleansed.

Perhaps the best example of the way in which
individual sinfulness has an effect on the whole people
is to be found in Joshua 7. After the fall of Jericho,
Joshua commanded that all living things should be killed
and all the treasures should be taken into the treasury
of the Lord's house. A man named Achan took some of
the treasures for himself and hid them.

We are told that as a result of his action the Israelites
were defeated at Ai. Joshua and the leaders spent a whole
day pleading with the Lord and seeking to discover the

reason for the calamity. 'Israel has sinned, they have
violated my covenant, which I commanded them to
keep,' said the Lord (Josh 7:11). Our twentieth-century
sense of justice baulks at this. It was Achan who sinned,
not the whole of Israel, so we want to ask, 'Why blame
them?'

In fact, they believed that his sin had tainted the whole
people, and therefore Israel as a whole had to pay for
the sin with their ignominious defeat. Achan, as an
individual, is eventually exposed and pays the price with
his life, and significantly, with the lives of his whole
family. Hence, his personal sin was seen as having a
devastating effect on the whole of Israel as well as himself
and his own family.

When we turn to the New Testament we find that
corporate sin—group sin—is still a significant factor.
When the Pharisees and Sadducees tried to test Jesus by
asking for a sign, his reply was damning: 'A wicked and
adulterous generation looks for a miraculous sign, but
none will be given it except the sign of Jonah' (Mt 16:4).
Jesus then warned against the 'yeast' of the Pharisees
and Sadducees, since they tainted the whole of society
in the same way that yeast affects the whole of the bread.

The Seventy-two were sent out by Jesus to the towns
and villages and he told them that they should not stay
in the town where they were not welcome: 'I tell you ,
it will be more bearable on that day for Sodom than for
that town' (Lk 10:1–12). As a result of the prominence
of the individual in our thinking today, we find the
thought of whole towns being condemned rather
strange. If someone were to say, 'Woe to Tamworth . . .',
we would immediately think, 'Wait a minute, there must
be many there who do not deserve to be condemned.'
But that is to miss Jesus' point—the sin of each individual
taints the whole.

Paul is also acutely aware of the corporate nature of sin. In 1 Corinthians 5 he is dealing with the report that a man is actually sleeping with his father's wife. As if that is not bad enough, the church has even colluded in this sin by not expelling him, and Paul's judgement is devastating: 'Hand this man over to Satan' (v5), which probably means, 'Exclude him (temporarily) from the fellowship of God's people'.

He then explains why it is dangerous to turn a blind eye to sin within the body: 'Don't you know that a little yeast works through the whole batch of dough? Get rid of the old yeast that you may be a new batch without yeast—as you really are' (vv 6–7).

In the Book of Revelation the judgements against the churches are both corporate and individual. For example, in Ephesus the whole church has lost the love for one another and for Christ:

> Yet I hold this against you: You have forsaken your first love. Remember the height from which you have fallen! Repent and do the things you did at first. If you do not repent, I will come to you and remove your lampstand from its place (Rev 2: 4–5).

But at Sardis, despite the condemnation that they are dead, there is this acknowledgement: 'Yet you have a few people in Sardis who have not soiled their clothes. They will walk with me, dressed in white, for they are worthy' (Rev 3:4). The emphasis here is on faithfulness. The process of affecting the whole, like yeast, can now work in reverse. All of the church can be influenced by the faithfulness of the few.

Sin, then, has two aspects in the Bible. It can be both corporate and individual. The individual's sin cannot be seen in isolation from the corporate and therefore, like the yeast in the dough, it can spread throughout, with devastating consequences for the whole group or society.

In the Old Testament we find another very significant factor in the interrelation of the individual and the whole group. There we find the leader representing the whole group before God. Time and time again Moses came before God to plead for the release of the people from condemnation and to ask God not to destroy them totally. The leader appointed by God, the individual, stands for the whole group and God heard his prayer.

Abraham also pleaded in a similar way for Sodom: 'The men turned away and went towards Sodom, but Abraham remained standing before the Lord' (Gen 18: 22). After a protracted negotiation with the Lord, he secured a most acceptable agreement—that if even ten righteous men were to be found in Sodom, the Lord would not destroy the city. Sadly the whole town was corrupt and therefore the destruction went ahead. The principle however, was clear—the leader has the function of representing the whole people before God.

Where do we see the collective nature of sin in the church today?

Money

Henry Chadwick in his book *The Early Church* (p 56) attributes the rapid growth of the the early church prior to Constantine to the incredible generosity and open-handedness of the churches:

> The practical application of charity was probably the most potent single cause of Christian success. The pagan comment 'See how these Christians love one another' (reported by Tertullian) was not irony. Christian charity expressed itself in care for the poor, for widows and

orphans, in visits to the brethren in prison or condemned to the living death of labour in the mines, and in social action in time of calamity like famine, earthquake, pestilence or war.

All of those actions must have been very costly in time, goods and money. It is a far cry from the record of the western churches of today! The financial response of so many churches to the needs of the world around and to the needs of those in desperate poverty abroad is shamefully low. Our own Diocesan World Mission Officer has pointed out that of the 460 parishes in our area, in any one year, between 150 and 170 give nothing to overseas mission. A further 70 give less than £20.00 per annum.

How often does the governing body of the church engage in double standards in regard to money? We say we just cannot afford a penny more for the needy, yet so often we seem to manage to find the money to do what we want to do, both as a church and as individuals. Who are the real givers in the church—is it the wealthy, or the poor?

We often think that our giving is so generous, yet in reality it can be pitiful. Very few indeed give until it hurts. There are few 'widow's mites' today. How often do we adopt without question society's standards concerning money—with all its secrecy, self-interest, and meanness? Where is our generosity to the poor? Where is our loving support for one another? Where is our ability to give and not to count the cost?

Of course, there are churches that are marvellous examples of God's generosity and love. Yet there are not many. Open-handedness is not one of our renowned characteristics! What is going on? It seems that we are

ensnared by corporate sin, we are bound up in the
world's values.

Idolatry

Usually when Christians consider the issue of idolatry,
a number of things are trotted out, such as money and
materialism, having a good time and so on. These of
course are relevant, but we believe that there is a much
more subtle kind of idolatry permeating the church,
which is to do with the 'spirit of the age'.

There is little doubt that the collapse of the nuclear
and extended family has had and is having very severe
repercussions on people's overall level of mental health
and wholeness. There is a tremendous need for security,
a need to have a place to feel safe, and a need to know
that while in that place all will be soothing and never
disturbing. The church, unwittingly perhaps, often
becomes that place and is then manipulated to fulfil those
needs.

The gospel is presented with little challenge, but the
maximum amount of comfort. Even the gifts of the Spirit
become abused and gifts such as prophecy are relegated
to the level of Christian sweeteners. Of course, we need
to hear we are loved, but we also need to hear that God
is moving us on, and in so doing sin must be addressed.
At a recent national conference on renewal, only one
prophecy out of about twenty given made any reference
to the pain that would have to be borne, and the
searching that would take place if righteousness is to be
established in the church and in the land. The rest were
soothing and affirming words of comfort. In one sense,
that is most encouraging, but the suspicion remains:
whose agenda is this—God's or ours?

In all churches in this country today there are
large numbers of people in pain. Several have

suffered unspeakable abuse in childhood, others were
systematically rejected and others rendered powerless
and unable to establish themselves in their world. It is
inevitable that the fears and the deep, unresolved needs
of such people will tend to set the hidden agenda for
the church, if those in fear and need are not confronted
openly with the challenge and opportunity for healing.

If these hurts are allowed to set the hidden agenda
for the church, it is inevitable that the gospel will be
modified. The people will then be affirmed in their
assumptions and left unchallenged. The structures
which they have set up to protect themselves from inner
conflict and pain will remain, and so the option for
healing will be consciously or unconsciously rejected.
This applies as much to the renewed churches as to the
traditional churches. The idol that is created is the big
'I': everything is orientated around me. I am the centre,
the worship must be to my liking, the preaching soothing
and entertaining, and the programmes of action enjoyable and fulfilling. But the essential purpose of the
church in meeting with its risen Lord is in danger of
being laid aside. How does the church meet our needs
without blunting the gospel's cutting edge?

So often security consists, not in launching out in faith
and 'walking on water', but rather in using my comfort
as the yardstick for what is acceptable in church life.
The consequences of this idolatry are to be seen all
around, particularly in the lack of impact that the church
has on society . If idolatry is going to be removed from
the church this will have to be addressed. There is, of
course, a fear of rocking the boat, a fear of persecution.
How can one move out when one is desperately trying
to assuage the pain inside? How can one take risks of
upsetting people when so many of them are already
hurting and when we are also so insecure in ourselves?

For the traditionalists, the fight is on to retain what is familiar, to feel comfortable in the surroundings and in the form of worship that never changes. For the 'renewed' church member, the aim is often to have a spiritual fix, an emotional high, that meets the needs inside. A good service is one that makes me feel good. In one sense it is no bad thing to feel uplifted after a service, but where this becomes the sole motivation, the focus is not on God and his requirements but on me and mine, and this is the essence of idolatry.

When we turn to the national scene, we see that the idolatry of the church has had devastating consequences throughout the centuries and has allowed the spread of the demonic on a huge scale.

John Dawson in his book *Taking Our Cities for God* (Word: 1991, p 150) has this to say:

> In human history it is easy to see the enemy coming in like a flood and the Lord raising up a standard against him. In a global sense, each generation faces Satan in the form of the spirit of antichrist or world domination. This is the spirit behind those who have ambition to rule the world, such as Napoleon or Hitler . . . a praying church should face this spirit and drive it off long before we find ourselves in a world at war.
>
> Physical violence represents an encroachment of spiritual violence into the material realm. The spirit of world domination can emerge only when the saints have lost their vigilance or when the international church has become severely divided over some issue.

If one looks at the history of the church in Germany prior to 1940, one can see how it had fallen into idolatry, or 'lost its vigilance', as Dawson would put it. The success of National Socialism and the election of Adolf Hitler was welcomed by many in the churches. The 1920s had seen a rise in decadence and corruption, due to economic collapse, and had scandalised church leaders of all traditions. After Hitler's Reichstag speech in March 1933 it was only a few months before a truce was signed between the Vatican and Hitler.

John Bowden in his book *Karl Barth* (p 64) summarises the state of the German church:

> From the 1920s onwards, groups of German Protestant pastors, who tended on the whole to be politically conservative, patriotic and paternalistic, had been binding themselves into associations aimed at giving a purely German characteristic to the Christian gospel. 'For a German,' one of the milder statements goes, 'the church is the community of believers who are obligated to fight for a Christian Germany.' Another statement indicates which of the last two words is meant to bear the main stress: 'A godless fellow-countryman is nearer to us than one of another race, even if he sings the same hymn or prays the same prayer.'

These groups of pastors rapidly became united, with an eventual national bishop approved by Hitler. This was, however, opposed by other groups in the church (Bonhoeffer and Niemoller being among them) which eventually became the Confessing Church.

Barth's comment was: 'In the last resort I saw my dear German people beginning to worship a false God . . .' (Bowden, op cit p 57).

The reasons for the idolatry were probably rooted in the pain of the 1920s—the saviour was seen as Hitler, not Jesus Christ. If Dawson is right, the idolatry of the church led to the appearance and power of Hitler, and the subsequent tragedy that engulfed the Jews and the whole world.

South Africa provides another example. Dawson has this to say:

Apartheid is a spirit, not just a political phenomenon. It is a spirit of tribalism and of racial separation that goes deep into African history. Apartheid has its roots in idolatry. When a good thing like family heritage is made into an idol, injustice results (op cit p 150).

What Dawson fails to mention is the part the Dutch Reformed Church played in this process. Trevor Huddleston in his book *Naught for Your Comfort* (Fount: 1977, p 63) outlines the theological stance of the Dutch Reformed Church, and describes it as 'sub-Christian'. He says:

Just as the children of Israel had a divine mission, a divinely given leadership which set them apart from and over against the indigenous peoples, the tribes they had met with and conquered—so the 'Afrikaner volk' also had its unique destiny on the continent of Africa. It is to be, for all time, the nation representing purity of race: whiteness, divinely ordained and given.

Trevor Huddleston goes on to describe a conversation between himself and a Afrikaner driver, who passionately believed in the necessity for apartheid. 'Our difference is eschatological,' said the driver. Huddleston comments that this is exactly right: 'The Dutch Reformed Church cannot conceive of a relationship between black and white *in this world*.' (Huddleston's italics.)

Now of course, at the time of writing we are seeing movement in the dismantling of apartheid, and the Dutch Reformed Church has modified its stance. It is interesting, though speculative, to ask how this kind of theology arose. To a degree, of course, it was always there. It was brought with the first settlers, but it was then honed to meet the needs of the time. Inevitably the first settlers and their families felt a sense of insecurity in their newly won territory. They knew they were settling on land which had not been theirs until now. Seeing themselves as the chosen people destined to inhabit the land gave them security and hope for the future. Tragically the security was given by a theology, a way of thinking, that gave them supremacy and a divine right to take the land. This was rejected by the vast majority of the Christian world.

Whenever we set up false beliefs for our own convenience and accredit them with God's authority, we move towards idolatry. The security is then in a belief structure, not in the risen Lord. The results of this process have been untold suffering for millions in our generation.

The failure of both the German church up to 1940 and of the Dutch Reformed Church in its early years in South Africa, to be Christ-centred, resulted in the nation and the church falling into idolatry. This in turn allowed full play to the demonic powers, with the suffering and chaos of which we are only too aware.

This is of course the basic pattern that we see particularly in the Old Testament. God is adapted to meet the needs of the people and idolatry results, with deadly consequences.

This is seen today at its most stark at a national level, but it is also seen at the local church level. The telltale signs include the lack of relevance of the church to the community, the double standards concerning money, the lack of charity, an overweening sense of its own importance, and a dramatic increase in people being caught up in the demonic. To address the issue at a local level, needs an understanding of how the demonic works in this situation.

The demonic at the local church level

If, for the sake of argument, we accept that there is such a thing as a demonic hierarchy and that there is a 'territorial spirit' for each area, it would make sense to suppose that there are other lesser spirits under it. If God allows demonisation because of our sinful rebellion against him, one would expect to see such demonisation taking place in areas of sin.

There may not however be such a close correlation as we might suppose. If a church is conniving in sin, such as idolatry, it renders itself ineffective in the proclamation of the gospel in any case. The demonic has no particular wish to repeat a task which we have obligingly already carried out ourselves! However if the issues of sinfulness are being addressed in the church, while there is still much to be dealt with, there is very often an upsurge in the demonic, or at least that has been our experience.

Why? Well, presumably the church has now become a battleground, since it is beginning to move out in the power of the gospel. The demonic now has a vested interest in keeping things as they were. Hence the battle now starts. At stake is not just an individual coming to healing and freedom but the general weakening of the hold of the demonic over the church and the area. In other words, the battle is strategic as well as individual. Church leaders need to bear this in mind, otherwise it is difficult at times to understand what is actually going on.

Is it not true that we simply need to address sin at an individual level and all will be well? In one sense, of course, this is correct: if all the individuals of the body of Christ were to confess their sins and repent, that would be all that needed to be done. However, this is unlikely to happen, since at any one time some will be repenting, some not, and some coming into repentance.

We have considered already the corporate nature of sin as seen in the Bible, and how it affects a community as a whole. We have also seen how Moses could act as the intercessor for the people because he was the leader of the people. In the same sense we believe the leaders of the church can address the issue of corporate sin, because they also represent the people. A word of caution, though, is necessary. In Chapter 3 we saw the hierarchical nature both of sin and the demonic. As one moves to address the corporate sin of the church, one is moving up the scale. As one moves up the scale of sin, so one has to be aware of the probability of moving up the scale of the demonic authority and power.

The demonic really does not like this, and the attempt will be made to try to keep the level of warfare at the individual level. Sadly, we fall for it! Leaders, time and time again, fail to address the corporate nature of sin, and leave the demonic strongholds of corporate sin in place.

Part of the reason for this is that often the leader himself or herself perpetuates the corporate sin by the manner of leadership he or she engages in. The leader's needs become the needs of the church. If a leader is deeply insecure, he or she will want to create a church that meets those needs in some way or another. The children of Israel built the golden calf with Aaron's blessing. Now it may be that he was simply too weak to stop them, but they still needed his connivance to go ahead. Leaders have a considerable influence over a church—more than is often realised—and need to acknowledge this fact if the body is to be cleansed.

Cleansing the leaders

Some time ago now we became very aware of this and realised that if we were to address the corporate nature of sin we would have to make a start with ourselves. The Lord started the process by giving a word to the leader of our intercessory prayer group.

It was a Thursday evening and Peter went along to the prayer group, as occasionally he did. He was delayed, and came in just when the worship was ending. The leader of the group then said that the Lord had laid on her heart Amos 7:8–9:

> And the Lord asked me, 'What do you see, Amos?' 'A plumb-line,' I replied. Then the Lord said, 'Look, I am setting a plumb-line among my people Israel; I will spare them no longer. The high places of Isaac will be destroyed and the sanctuaries of Israel will be ruined; with my sword I will rise against the house of Jeroboam.

Both John and Peter had become aware, over the previous weeks, of deep pain that needed healing— things that happened in the past, mainly in childhood, were erupting and causing problems in the present. We were also both aware that these deep pains had affected the way that we did things in the parish, and that our security, to a large extent, rested on soothing these pains! God was saying, 'Enough is enough!' It was also almost as though God was saying 'Become aware of what is going on inside you and how you relate to others, and the effect this is having throughout the church.' We decided to receive ministry.

At the time of writing it is continuing, and will probably do so for a long time! Healing has not been instantaneous, but recognition of the areas of pain has allowed us to see what is happening. It has been very

painful but we have sought to be obedient to God in this
and we have seen a release of his blessings upon the
church.

It took some time for us to see that God was dealing
with a large number of leaders in this way. We were not
the only ones! There was a pattern to all of this, and it
was spreading through the church. The strongholds of
security that were based not on God but on our
inner needs were being healed. We were beginning to
recognise our own spiritual poverty and the truth of
Jesus' words: 'Unless you change and become like little
children, you will never enter the kingdom of heaven'
(Mt 18:3). God was destroying the idolatry of false
security.

Leaders must face up to the truth of where they are,
what their agenda really is and why, and what healing
they and their fellow-leaders require, if the body is to be
cleansed.

Cleansing the body

Any attempt at cleansing the body that does not start
with the leaders is doomed to failure. People have to see
that God is leading, and witness the fruit in the leaders'
lives. Whenever someone says, 'I feel the Lord is calling
the church to repentance', we need to see that this
message will only carry conviction if the process starts
with the one who brings it!

Congregations are rightly cautious when called to
undertake some activity by their leadership. They don't
like signing blank cheques. The credibility gap of the
leadership will be measured to the last inch, and if it is
found to be too large, church members will regard any
call to action with suspicion. They will say, 'If we as a

congregation are going to be cleansed and healed by God, let's see it start with the leaders!'

This process, then, must start with truth.

Truth

> We know also that the Son of God has come and has given us understanding, so that we may know him who is true. And we are in him who is true—even in his Son Jesus Christ. He is the true God and eternal life. Dear children, keep yourselves from idols (1 Jn 5:21–22).

If the credibility gap between what the leader is and what he preaches has been reduced as a result of personal obedience, then the body will begin to hear the truth. The truth has to be spelt out concerning corporate sin:

1. No one is a spiritual island—you cannot sin privately! Your sin is not just your own concern, but rather it affects the whole body.
2. Corporate sin must be highlighted and owned by the body. There must be clear teaching, for example, on what idolatry is, how it comes about and how we all get involved in it.
3. Words of confession are not enough—there has to be real repentance. For repentance to take place, an actual turning round, the root causes must be addressed. If it is some form of idolatry, the pains of the past will probably have to be acknowledged and brought for healing. There must be spiritual reality, not wishful thinking.

It is at this point that individuals sometimes experience demonic interference. We have noted time and time again how the demonic twists and inflames our psychologically weak areas. It has one beneficial effect, of course—it pinpoints the areas of need. This is an area which needs very careful discernment. It takes time and practice to discern what is demonic and what is inner pain. It is very easy to jump too quickly to one conclusion or another. We must always proceed with caution. (See Chapter 6 'Cleansing The Individual'.)

We have seen three reactions to this process of cleansing the body. First, there are those who know what we are talking about and immediately hear God and are prepared to deal with the problem. Secondly, there are those who know that something is wrong but cannot pinpoint it. This is often cleared up with prayer and ministry. Thirdly, there are those who simply do not know what we are saying. Getting to these people is most easily done by pointing to their relationships and to the fruit of their interactions with other people. It needs a great deal of honesty and truth.

This applies equally to other areas of life where we collude with each other in sinful attitudes—for example, our approach to the issue of money. It is clear in the level of giving week by week whether people are being obedient or not. Some churches, such as the Vineyard Churches, deal with this in a radical manner. You simply cannot be a leader unless you tithe! This is all very well, if you begin at this point, but most churches do not. Bringing whole churches to realise that they do not deal honestly with God in the matter of giving, needs systematic teaching and firm determination to deal at all times in the world of reality. This involves a refusal to join in the corporate collusion that we are all poor and cannot afford to be more generous.

4. Once the corporate sin has been acknowledged and dealt with, in the first instance by the leaders, one can then move on to the issue of cleansing the Body from

unreality which is in turn aggravated by the demonic. It is extremely unlikely that the church will be able to move in unison on this issue, since there will always be people at different stages. It is therefore the responsibility of the leaders regularly to bring the issue before the membership at appropriate times.

Cleansing from demonic influence

The temptation here is to deal with the issue as quickly as possible and with little forethought or consideration of what is involved.

At one time one of the leaders of the church had a picture of our church surrounded by three bands of steel. By addressing the demonic in one area (see Chapter 8) one band was released, yet there were still two bands left. We feel fairly certain that these represent money and idolatry, but we have not addressed them as yet— why?

First, the leadership across the church must see the issues and be prepared to face them. If this is not done, any repentance fails to get to grips with the roots of the problem. This is happening gradually, but we do not feel that as yet the time is right for a frontal assault. Secondly, as the leaders pray about it God does not seem to be indicating that the time has come to face the issues.

The initial principle, then, in cleansing the body from demonic influence is that the sin and areas of rebellion in the leadership must first be addressed, and God must be allowed to direct the timing of this. The danger of being premature is that the results will not be lasting unless we become fully aware of the area of sin which needs to be repented of and renounced.

We have found that applying the following principles has been helpful when the time seems right to proceed:

1. Take time. The leaders need to take time out—maybe a day, maybe more.
2. Begin with praise and worship. Affirm the goodness and triumph of God. Affirm what he has given us, and the fact that we are heirs with his Son.
3. Review the situation before God.
4. Confess personal sins and the corporate sins of the leadership team, and receive God's forgiveness.
5. Bring the sins of the body before the Lord. Repent for the body, ask for God's forgiveness and seek the restoration of his mercy and grace.
6. Command in the Lord's name, that all demonic influence upon the body be uprooted and be gone.

8

Spiritual Warfare : Attack

The driving out of an evil spirit in Capernaum is Christ's first miracle recorded in Mark's Gospel (Mk 1: 21–28). At the very start of Jesus' public ministry in Matthew, he is led into the desert to be tempted by Satan (Mt 3:1–11). Luke has the same account as Jesus' work begins. Is it just coincidence that in each of the Synoptic Gospels the public ministry of Christ starts with a confrontation with the demonic?

We would say emphatically—*No*! James Dunn in *Jesus and the Spirit* (p48) has this to say about Jesus' contact with the demonic:

> Jesus saw his exorcisms not merely as the healing of demented people, not merely as the casting out of demons, not merely as a victory over Satan, but as the binding of the powers of evil that was looked for at the end of the age. The final battle was already joined and Satan already being routed.

The fact that the first three Gospels all open Jesus' public ministry with demonic encounters is important. Jesus was proclaiming the final victory and it was a victory which clearly included the conquest of Satan and the powers of evil.

Generally the vast majority of the church relegate this

warfare to the bottom or near the bottom of the agenda. This is, we suggest, contrary to the teaching and example of Jesus as seen in the New Testament. It is often fear which causes church leaders to be wary of this whole subject—fear of the unknown. Certainly we would agree that caution is essential. However, many important functions in life contain an element of risk, yet fear of an accident does not stop us crossing the road. Risk, in itself, is not a sufficiently good reason for avoiding the situation.

Doing battle with Satan and his minions, we would claim, is essential for the spread of the kingdom of God. In fact, to spread the kingdom of God is to destroy the kingdom of darkness which has held people in its grip. To be authorised and empowered by the Lord to fulfil the Great Commission (ie, to go and make disciples of all nations) is to be empowered to engage in spiritual warfare. You cannot have one without the other.

The question arises as to whether those churches that are experiencing problems, and finding the gospel falls on deaf ears, are taking spiritual warfare seriously. It is quite possible that this is where the problem is rooted and that this significantly contributes to the lack of success in making disciples. Unless the church takes spiritual warfare seriously at a personal and corporate level, this Decade of Evangelism is doomed to failure since the vital issues will only be half addressed.

A number of years ago Peter went to a conference just outside Durham. It was an off-shoot of the Wimber conferences at that time, led by a young pastor called Steve Nicholson, who was obviously a gifted pastor and teacher. It was a very formative time for Peter and so it was with great interest that he read an account of Steve's church in Evaston, Illinois, in Peter Wagner's book *Territorial Spirits* (p 31):

Steve Nicholson has preached the gospel in the area for six years, with virtually no fruit. He and the members of his church pray for the sick and a few get well. But his Vineyard Christian Fellowship is not growing. Nicholson begins some serious prayer and fasting. A grotesque unnatural being appears to him. It growls, 'Why are you bothering me?' It identifies itself as the demon of witchcraft who has dominion over the geographical area.

In the heat of warfare, Nicholson names the city streets in the surrounding area. The spirit retorts, 'I don't want to give you that much.' In the name of Jesus, Nicholson commands the spirit to give up the territory.

During the next three months the church doubles in size from 70 to 150, mostly from new converts coming out of witchcraft. Nearly all of the new believers must be delivered from demons.

At St Editha's we have seen church growth partly, we believe, as a result of taking warfare seriously. For the most part this has involved ministry to individuals, but rapidly a new front is opening up before us. This is in the realm of ministry concerning corporate structures and activities. As we have wrestled with these issues we have found certain principles to be be essential for the task.

Power

There is a real problem with language here. The very concept of spiritual warfare waged in power raises all kinds of preconceived notions. Our minds flit to the usual understanding of power games: to win is the aim, to have more power than the other side is the goal. Yet the New Testament understanding of power exemplified in Jesus turns our usual understanding of power on its head. It is a far cry from the 'get up and sock them 'concept of power.

We see real power in Jesus on the cross: 'And having disarmed the powers and authorities, he made a public spectacle of them, triumphing over them by the cross' (Col 2:15).

The cross is the triumph of God's love for us . The powers were broken, not by a spectacular show of brute force, but as a result of Jesus' utter obedience to the Father and his willingness to die for us: 'Hands that flung stars into space, to cruel nails surrendered' (Graham Kendrick in his song 'The Servant King').

Christ was well able to overcome with sheer power, and yet he chose the way of suffering in obedience to the Father in order to rout Satan and to set us free. God loved us so much. Here we see the pattern for Christian action. We are not to seek worldly power and influence and bring God's wishes into being by overwhelming fire-power but by learning to love and to utterly trust God. We too are to walk the path of obedient humility and, paradoxically, in so doing we shall see the power of God working through us in amazing ways.

The weapons of victory

Knowing where you stand

Generally speaking, we are not good at living in the reality of what we have been given in Christ, and we fail to understand the true nature and strength of the church.

C.S. Lewis in his book *The Screwtape Letters* (Fount: 1982, p14) makes the point clearly. Screwtape (a high demon) is writing to his trainee demon:

One of our great allies at present is the Church itself. Do not misunderstand me. I do not mean the Church as we see her spread out through all time and space and rooted in eternity, terrible as an army with banners. That, I confess, is a spectacle which makes our boldest tempters uneasy. But fortunately it is quite invisible to these humans. All your patient sees is the half-finished, sham Gothic erection on the new building estate.

We have great difficulty hearing with confidence what is plainly set out in Scripture: 'For in Christ all the fulness of the Deity lives in bodily form, and you have been given fulness in Christ, who is the head over every power and authority' (Col 2:9). 'Now if we are children, then we are heirs—heirs of God and co-heirs with Christ . . .' (Rom 8:17).

The consequences of this are phenomenal: the authority and power of Jesus are ours. But this is not unconditional; Romans 8:17 continues : '. . . if indeed we share in his sufferings in order that we may also share in his glory.'

The authority and power we receive are conditional on our remaining in Christ and being obedient, even if it means suffering. Scripture is clear that this will be the case.

When Jesus prayed for all believers in John 17, he said, 'I have given them the glory that you gave me, that they may be one as we are one' (Jn 17:22). What an amazing thought—Jesus has given his glory to us! This is not all; with it goes the tremendous promise of power: 'And I will do whatever you ask in my name, so that the Son may bring glory to the Father' (Jn 14:13).

When we respond, then, to God in faith and obedience, the power of God is clearly evident: 'I tell you the truth, anyone who has faith in me will do what I have been doing' (Jn 14:12). This power is without measure because it is the power of God himself.

This is part of the inheritance that we have been given

by God and yet, sadly, it is an inheritance that we
continually fail to accept fully. One of the hardest words
that we heard in the writing of this book was the comment
made by someone coming out of satanism: 'The church
is powerless, because they do not live in their inheritance.'

Prayer

'Pray in the Spirit on all occasions with all kinds of prayers
and requests'(Eph 6:18).

One of the ways that Satan suffocates churches is by
seeking to destroy prayer which really communicates
with God. Without such prayer there is no battle.

Jesus says 'I tell you the truth, the Son can do nothing
by himself; he can only do what he sees the Father doing,
because whatever the Father does the Son also does'
(Jn 5:19). Jesus sees what the Father does because he
knows the Father, and that knowledge comes through
constant prayer. It is prayer characterised by closeness.
Jesus calls God 'Abba'—'Daddy'. It scandalised the
religious authorities of the time, but we are called into
that same relationship.

As we draw close to our Father in prayer, we learn to
hear what he wants of us. We also see where he wants
us to go. We can be assured that our walk in this direction
will be empowered by God and will lead to victory. If
this closeness to God is absent at an individual as well as
at a corporate level, there can be no warfare. Warfare is
doing obediently what the Father says because it is only
there that we move in his victory and power. To go
anywhere else is to invite trouble!

Praise and worship.

Praise and worship have astonishing effects. In Acts
16:16–25, Paul and Silas were stripped and beaten after
ministering to a slave girl. Some thanks for disposing of

a spirit of divination! They were taken off to prison where immediately they praise God and pray. There follows an earthquake and the net result is that the jailer comes to faith, along with his household.

In Joshua 6:1–27, we read of Joshua taking the city of Jericho. Who first marched round the walls? Amazingly, we hear that it is the priests with trumpets, followed by the ark. Not many armies today send the chaplains with the regimental band into battle first. Yet the praise of God is more powerful than any military hardware.

In Joshua 3, the children of Israel cross the Jordan, and again the ark and the priests go first. It seems bizarre to send the ark into flood water, but that is what God commanded. Where praise and worship take place, there God is invited to draw near to his people. It is a meeting in vulnerability and openness, and encountering God afresh. This puts God at the forefront—like the ark. Praise and worship allow us to see with God's eyes, to see what he really wants. As we worship, we let go of our defective vision and begin to grasp the vision of God. In warfare this is absolutely critical, since it is so easy to become preoccupied with our fears and limited understanding.

The word of God

In Ephesians 6:17 we read: 'Take the helmet of salvation and the sword of the Spirit, which is the word of God.' What is meant here by the word of God? There are two aspects to be considered.

First, the written words in the Bible are 'the word of God'. In Luke 4:1–13, Jesus uses Scripture as a weapon against Satan: 'It is written: 'worship the Lord your God and serve him only''' (v8).

However, Satan also uses Scripture, 'For it is written:

"He will command his angels concerning you . . ."' (v 10).

It is therefore not enough simply to say that the Bible is 'the sword of the Spirit'. If that were the case, why is it that Satan uses Scripture? Obviously there is more to it than that.

The second aspect is that of the 'word of God' as the empowered word of God.   'And God said, '"Let there be light, and there was light' (Gen 1:3). His very word contained such authority and power that when it was spoken, it happened.

In the Bible we have the inspired and authoritative word of God. It has stood the test of time and is quite unique. Yet it is a mistake to use it as a talisman, containing power within itself, so that if you quote it, it happens. That is more akin to superstition than godliness.

The authority of the Bible is not intrinsic, but a reality that exists because of the living relationship between the written word (the Bible) and the living Word, God himself. That means that Scripture cannot be applied outside of that relationship with God and be considered to be the sword of the Spirit. Indeed, Satan's quoting of Scripture contained no such authority.

The very wording that Paul gives should point us to this understanding: it is the sword of the *spirit*. It is the Holy Spirit of God that empowers the written word to be the living word. No co-operation with the Holy Spirit, no sword of the Spirit!

When Paul wrote his letter of the Ephesians, the New Testament had not yet been put together as we know it now. So when he referred to the word of God, was he referring just to the Old Testament? Yes, he was in part, but Paul was very well aware of the double dynamic of the written word and the Spirit. He was well aware that

God speaks now and this played a major part in his thinking.

Likewise every Christian who believes God speaks to them in prayer must have some knowledge of how God operates in this twofold way.

The two forms of understanding, the written word and the Spirit, are, of course, totally interrelated. To have prophecy that is contrary to the biblical witness is obviously wrong. To have a superstitious, talisman-like belief in the written word, is equally wrong. The word of God is the written word empowered by the Spirit of God: the two must go together, the Holy Spirit and the Bible.

In spiritual warfare we need to be reliant on God to lead us to see what we are dealing with. To be reliant means of necessity to hear God, using the gifts of the Spirit (discernment, prophecy, words of knowledge, etc), but these must be in line with the written biblical record. One is the safeguard for the other. If the Bible is ignored then the possibilities for deception are endless. If the Spirit is ignored, the ministry becomes arid, lifeless and lacking in authority.

Warfare is about taking the victory where it has already been won by Jesus Christ. To do so we have the ultimate weapon, the sword of the Spirit, which is the word of God.

Warfare as the body of Christ

Most people are introduced to spiritual warfare as a result of an appeal for help from an individual who is in great need. However, warfare is conducted not only at an individual level, but also at a corporate level. In 1 Corinthians 12:12–30, Paul lays out the nature of the body of Christ. In verse 27 he says: 'Now you are the body of Christ, and each one of you is a part of it.' It is a body that works together, or should do!

It is essential that all forms of warfare should be conducted in a cohesive and co-ordinated fashion. To use a military example:' suppose one has superb individual troops, with a high level of physical fitness, training skill and experience. If these men are each left to do battle from their own positions, with little reference to what the others are doing, problems will soon arise. The lack of co-ordination will surely lead to heavy casualties. An army is no place for un-coordinated individual action! Planning, communication and corporate action are needed if the battle is to be won.

This raises the question of how this is to be done. Co-ordination implies that someone must be the co-ordinator, which brings us to the question of leadership and authority.

Authority and role of the leader

The church which Peter attended in Durham while training for the ordained ministry of the Church of England, underwent a number of upheavals. The former vicar had retired and a new vicar was to be appointed. In the meantime the congregation assumed that pastoral care was to be taken up by the 'elders' who were also lay readers. However, the diocesan authorities decided that they would withdraw all the readers' licences. There was quite suddenly no authority structure in the church. The results were traumatic, not least for those who had lost their licences. The authorities had effectively said their ministries were no longer recognised.

This action had major consequences for that church. Prior to this event the church had been known as a leading church in renewal. It had a well developed teaching and healing ministry and had run many day conferences in local churches. Suddenly the ministry seemed to have lost its validity, because there was no authority structure in which it could operate.

In the end it was felt that this ministry was of God and needed to continue. To enable it to continue, strenuous efforts were made to base it at a local church under church authority, as well as having a degree of autonomy.

Robert Runcie in *Authority in Crisis* (SCM Press: 1988, p 22) says:

> Christians must start with the inevitability of authority. To believe in God, the ultimate reality, is to believe in the authority of God. To believe in Jesus as the Word made flesh is to believe that the man Jesus Christ uniquely communicates the authority of God. To believe that the crucified Christ lives is to believe that his unique communication of the authority of God continues to be heard. To belong to the church is to believe that this is the locus where the word of God is authentically preached.

Authority and the right understanding of authority are critical to the welfare of the church. The full authority of God is invested in the church as the body, with Christ as the head. In spiritual warfare this becomes critically important.

In Peter's recognition of Jesus as the Messiah (Mt 16:13–20) we see three main principles:

1. The confirmation that the Messiah (the Christ) has indeed come: 'You are the Christ, the Son of the living God.' Because Christ has come, the church is established under his authority and headship.
2. It is an authority that is given to the church but it still remains God's authority: 'And I tell you that you are

Peter, and on this rock I will build my church, and the gates of Hades will not overcome it.' Peter is assisting in building God's church, not his own, and it remains God's church. God is building it, not Peter.

3. I will give you the keys of the kingdom of heaven; whatever you bind on earth will be bound in heaven, and whatever you loose on earth will be loosed in heaven.' The more accurate Greek translation is: 'Whatever you bind on earth will have been bound in heaven, and whatever you loose on earth will have been loosed in heaven.'

In other words there is a co-ordination going on between heaven and earth. The authority that is coming into play is not the authority of the individual but God's authority, working through that person. The authority of God given to the church is not a commodity that is owned by any individual or group, but God's authority imparted as part of the living relationship between God and the church.

In order for authority to be effective it needs to be recognised and obeyed. If it is not obeyed it is not, as far as that individual is concerned, effective authority. Obedience is therefore a vital factor in the whole issue of authority. The primary sin of Adam and the whole human race is rebellion against God by rejecting his authority.

For any organisation to function efficiently it must have leadership. Within the Christian church, leadership is not a function of power or of status but of gifting. It is a gift given by the Holy Spirit. Paul says, '[If a man's gift] is leadership, let him govern diligently' (Rom 12:8).

The structure of leadership is not our concern here, but rather the principles behind that leadership. If we believe that God has called certain people to be leaders in a particular church, then we need to understand that ministering without their approval is, in effect, a rebellion against God's leadership, and is therefore sin.

This is not to advocate wholesale unthinking obedience, but to recognise that spiritual warfare cannot be undertaken without the authority of God. 'No one is an island' in the Christian life, therefore every action has consequences for others. If one undertakes warfare without the approval of God's appointed leaders, one is not operating with the authority of God. The possibilities then for destruction are limitless.

Michael Harper in his book *Let My People Grow* (Hodder, 1977, p 100) rightly says:

> The church can only recognise those whom God has authorised, and can only recognise those whom God has gifted and empowered. No amount of theological training or human pressure can bestow charisma on a person. It is the sole gift of God ... and without charisma, however learned ministers may be, however dedicated, and however many of the right hands have been laid on them, their work will be a failure.

Leaders must be leaders, and the church has a responsibility to ensure that this is the case. We must include here that it is possible to turn down the gifts of God. We have come across leaders who are gifted by God, but for one reason or another have not picked up their gifting, or have laid it aside. Conversely, we have come across leaders who are not gifted by God.

We have all probably seen churches where everything runs smoothly while the leader is present, but gets into trouble when he moves on to another job, or even when he simply goes on his annual holiday. Many churches have a pyramid structure of leadership, where one person is ultimately responsible for all areas of church life. Whether this pattern is right or wrong, its workability will depend on how authority is delegated.

The structure at St Editha's is indeed something of a pyramid with John, the Vicar, at the top. We soon began to recognise a pattern of problems every time John went away, despite the fact that Peter was competent at handling most of the situations which arose.

As soon as John and family packed their suitcases, put their bouncy retriever into the car and towed their caravan out of Tamworth heading for some delightful spot on the coast, the trouble would start. A crop of relationship problems would spring up in the church family, phone calls would pour in from non-church members with tales of ghosts and poltergeists. Attacks on the leadership would suddenly arise. Church members would experience demonic attacks and need ministry 'immediately', and disorganisation ruled.

We decided that this was not just a case of playing up while the boss was away, but that it had a definite demonic element. An experiment seemed a good idea. John was due for a sabbatical (well, one needs time to write a book!), so at his last service for three months he gave the authority for leading the church to Peter, and promptly disappeared to France. The results spoke for themselves. To Peter's immense relief, parish life continued smoothly.

Authority has a double edge. It has to be given by God on the one hand, and recognised and obeyed by man on the other. In the case of John publicly handing over authority to Peter, this was done. It was a public act, in the name of God, which was assented to by those present. (If there were any objections they were not voiced!)

Sometimes this double edge is not recognised. A person can be placed in a position of authority without him or her having been given the gift of leadership by God. At other times, God-given leadership is not recognised by man. In churches that delegate leadership, a common problem is to give responsibility without authority, and that just leads to frustration!

For effective warfare there has to be effective leadership which is God-given and recognised by man.

Strategic warfare

How is the church supposed to engage in warfare? When we started in spiritual warfare, we were mainly engaged in ministering to individuals. No sooner was one person sorted out than another appeared in similar need. At times it got so hectic that it felt as if we were being given the runaround. We would go to bed shattered and our wives and families were beginning to wonder whether they actually had husbands or lodgers. The situation seemed to be getting out of control. How could this be what God wanted? In some ways, it felt good; here we were doing what Jesus commanded, seeing tremendous results. Yet we were putting our families under intolerable strains. Something had to change.

Planning

The idea of planning does not sit very easily with a number of church ministers. We can plan Sunday schools, events, fund raising and so on, yet we are sometimes very reluctant to plan strategically to reach spiritual objectives. 'You will quench the Spirit, you will stop freedom' was a comment often heard.

We were forced into planning by our hard-pressed situation; we *had* to start thinking and acting strategically. Does the Lord really want this? We are convinced that he does. Spiritual warfare is one of the most demanding of ministries and is physically and emotionally draining. One becomes overwhelmed unless planning takes place. Indeed that is part of what Satan wants. The more tired one gets, the less clearly one thinks, and the more vulnerable one becomes. Inevitably, as it goes on less time is spent in prayer and waiting on the Lord.

The biblical witness

God is a God of planning. Ephesians 1:3–14, sets out God's planning. It was no spur of the moment decision that Christ came, it was planned:

> In him we were also chosen, having been predestined according to the plan of him who works out everything in conformity with the purpose of his will, in order that we, who were the first to hope in Christ, might be for the praise of his glory (vv 11–12).

'The Lord Almighty has sworn "Surely, as I have planned, so it will be, and as I have purposed, so it will stand"' (Is 14:24). We cannot imagine God acting in a haphazard fashion. He plans ahead, and so it follows that we should lay plans in accordance with God's plan.

David operated according to this principle when he built the Temple: 'All this is in writing,' David said, "because the hand of the Lord was upon me, and he gave me understanding in all the details of the plan"' (1 Chron 28:19).

To know God's plan for us we need to set aside time to listen to him in prayer and study. Looking at the many examples of God's planning in the Bible makes an illuminating study in itself. Paul carefully planned his journeys in accordance with God's plan: 'When I planned this, did I do it lightly? Or do I make my plans in a worldly manner so that in the same breath I say "yes, yes" and "No, no"?' (2 Cor 1:17).

Sometimes we hear God incorrectly and the plans we make turn out to be wrong. This does not mean that we should abandon all planning, but it does mean we have to get back on our knees and learn how to hear more accurately.

Where do we start?

Prayerfully set out the objectives How big does God want the church? What kind of age groups? What ministries does God want in the church? God has a particular plan for each church. No church can cover all the needs of a particular community. Different churches have different strengths, and God does not usually ask a church to major in every area of ministry.

Where are we now? What is our real situation? Is our Sunday school really a creche? For whose benefit is the worship? What kind of leadership do we have; is it shared in name or in reality; who makes the decisions?

What do we need to do to get to the objectives God has given us? In other words, how do we get from where we are to where God is planning for us to be? There may be many stages along the way, and we may not see all of those at the outset. We particularly need to ask God to show us where to start. He may possibly want us to begin with only one small area of church life. At each step we will need prayerfully to ask God: is this the right direction? If our church seats 200, and God is planning for a church initially of 50–150 people over the next five years, there is little point in planning for a new extension.

This kind of forward looking is commonplace in business, but often it is alien to the church and feels uncomfortable. However, God seems to be prompting his church into more attentive listening and more careful planning.

As we see what kind of church God wants, we can start to address the specific areas of ministry that are important in his plan. God will provide the resources for his plan. That is certainly our experience.

Some time ago we knew God was asking us to provide a service for young families. It would need to be one at which they would feel comfortable, where noise would not matter, and where they could hear the gospel in a way that they could understand. Our resources were limited, so we started to pray particularly for a music group. Within three months God brought in the people required. Our music group was up and running. It was in his will.

Planning spiritual warfare

A similar approach is needed in the area of spiritual warfare.

1. We need to deal in reality. We cannot overstress this. Satan loves to deal in lies and to encourage the church to deal in make-believe. Unless the emphasis starts where we actually are the result can be chaotic.
2. As we have seen in previous chapters, most churches have open doors to the demonic. The initial teaching must address this, often at very fundamental levels. We must rediscover the significance of the victory of the cross and its relevance to spiritual warfare. We must know what it is to be actually forgiven. We must have the gospel proclaimed in its fullness. Repentance and holiness must be high on the agenda. Worship

must be taught, and openness to the Lord developed. This is the starting point; it may sound elementary, but it is necessary.

3. We need to raise awareness of the realities of spiritual warfare as laid out in the Bible. This may well be a two-year programme, but it should not be rushed. Having made a degree of progress with this, we find there is a difficulty. Public teaching about spiritual warfare, beyond the basics, is rather unwise if one has new people continually coming into the church. Further teaching is given as appropriate in group situations. This programme is ongoing, as is the process of recognising the different gifts and ministries given by God in this field. It is essential that all this is undergirded with prayer.

As we continued in the ministry to individuals in the church concerning the demonic, we became aware that there were different layers to spiritual warfare. The awareness started first of all in small ways. For example, one member of the congregation used to live outside Tamworth and commute in to church. As he came into the town, he often experienced intense headaches and a deadness. There was obviously pollution in the air! Or was there?

We also noted that when praying for release from oppression with some individuals, there seemed to be a dominant oppressive presence. When this was dealt with, the additional oppressive problems ceased. After due reflection, prayer and study we decided that there was probably something in this business of territorial spirits that needed addressing. It was very much a case of 'faith seeking understanding'.

For the first step we decided to ask the regular weekly prayer group to pray about this area. They seemed to perceive there was demonic oppression of specific kinds concentrated in different parts of the town. To a degree these were fairly predictable—for example, they discerned a spirit of lust in the locality of the night-clubs. This was then followed up with a group consisting of ourselves and another church praying at the various places in the town which the Lord seemed to indicate.

However, we did not feel that we had got to the bottom of the matter, and the Lord seemed to be saying there was more. So we decided we would get together those who led the ministry teams and those with a ministry of prophecy, to start praying about this and attempt to discover what the Lord was saying.

The meeting took place on a Saturday morning, and will remain etched on Peter's memory for years to come. There were only four people present. They were a little apprehensive, but generally excited about what the Lord seemed to be calling them to do. Three had arrived and were awaiting Kate (who is often used in a prophetic ministry). Suddenly the door burst open and Kate came into the room, looking very white and shaken.

They sat her down and asked her what had happened. After a strong cup of tea she was sufficiently composed to be able to tell us: 'I was driving along the road when suddenly the car began to swerve towards the oncoming traffic. I heaved with all my might on the steering-wheel and only just managed to get it back and avoid an accident.'

The first thought was that perhaps the steering was faulty, but a careful check by the person who maintained the car revealed no mechanical defect. To this day there has been no further incident with that car. They had to take seriously the fact that the episode could well be related to the meeting.

The atmosphere of the meeting underwent a sudden change. There was life-threatening malevolence here. This was no minor incident. They started with praise, praise for the Lord's protection and care, and praise that he does indeed have the victory over the demonic. Then they started to pray for the town asking the Lord to show them the name and nature of the territorial spirit. The Lord seemed to show them that there was a spirit of destruction over the place. So they prayed against that spirit, asking the Lord to lift that spirit off the town. Still there was a sense that the issue was not resolved.

They asked the Lord to show them whether there was anything more he wanted them to do. The answer was affirmative, but they were not to go any further in prayer. This seemed a bit strange, so they discussed it and prayed about not praying any more about it(!). The issue, they began to see, was about holiness. It was almost as if God would not allow them to go any further until they sorted out their own lives. God seemed to be saying that if they wished to continue in this they must radically grow in holiness.

Two or three weeks later Peter felt that they needed to go round the church again, praying and cleansing the building. When they started they suddenly realised that God was asking them to come against the spirit of destruction once again that was rooted in the church. They thought they had dealt with him once, and yet here he was again! So they went round the church, repenting of all the sin down the ages that God brought to mind. There was plenty of it! And they claimed the ground, telling the spirit of destruction to flee. The results of this were astonishing, not least because they occurred in a totally unexpected way. For the six months prior to this event there were two full-time youth workers with the church, and they had spent a proportion of their time out on the streets, talking to young people about the gospel. The response on the street had been lukewarm. When they went out on Saturday night that week, sixteen young people wanted to know about the gospel.

This drew our attention once again to the realities of the situation: the streets of our town and indeed the whole world are God's and under the lordship of Christ. The prince of this world, Satan, stood condemned at Christ's coming (Jn 16:11) and, as a result of his ministry and victory on the cross, we are assured by Jesus that '. . . now the prince of this world will be driven out' (Jn 12:31). This means that any claim by a demonic spirit to 'own' territory is bogus. We have the right to claim the streets of the town in the name of Christ and for Christ.

However, the experiences of dealing with the territorial spirit convinced us that we needed a more systematic way of handling this issue. It was obviously going to be time-consuming, and therefore we felt that we needed a more comprehensive plan. But how were we to do this?

The prayer group

Two to three months prior to these events a couple, Susie and Clive, had joined the church. They felt that God was calling them to spiritual warfare. They were mature Christians and had previously been involved in the intercessory ministry. It seemed that God was providing the means. We needed a group who were specifically called to this ministry, not just to deal with the issue of territorial spirits, but also to provide a network of prayer that could be called into action with a phone call, if the need arose.

They were to provide prayer cover for deliverance ministry in the parish as well as seek to discern what the Lord was saying about specific situations.

We felt from the very beginning that there had to be a specific calling to any individuals who might be involved in this work. Being in the front line of a battle is a tough place to be, and our experiences of the enemy so far told us to expect problems with relationships and communication. We knew every effort would be made to destroy this group. So the members of the group had to have the assurance that they were called by God, so that hopefully they could ride out the storms as they arose.

The Lord mercifully made it clear who was to be involved. We started with a list ,and it was gradually whittled down to those who had a strong sense that God was calling them. With some, though not all, it was very encouraging to find that the Lord had gone before and that they were just waiting for the phone call.

The prayer group was in place—or so we thought! The very first meeting was a disaster. Everyone felt heavy, confused and not a little upset. Something was clearly wrong.

We had very carefully chosen a room in the church to which no one had access except this group. Unfortunately we had inadvertently chosen the one place in the church that had not been regularly prayed in or cleansed! The group prayed for the room but it did not seem to make much difference.

The day after the meeting Peter received a phone call from Clive, who was very upset. What was going on, he wanted to know? The more they talked, the more Peter felt that they had come across this before. It sounded suspiciously like the spirit of destruction again. Somewhat irreverently, they joked that it was as if he had been ousted from everywhere else but had come to roost in this room. That might well be not far from the truth!

Peter felt that they should meet all together in the room and celebrate communion there, that being a vivid reminder and proclamation of the victory of Christ. Together they expressed repentance over the sins of ages past. The sense of praise and worship grew and there was a tremendous awareness of the victory of the Lord. The spirit of destruction was duly dispatched into the hands of God and a great sense of peace and the Lord's presence came on the room.

The group at the time of writing is still in action and has proved itself invaluable in many ways. This is one of the specific structures God asked us to put in place. It may not, however, be required in every locality, but it remains a possibility.

To date the group has been primarily dealing with situations as they arise. We pray and trust that this is a vital step in taking on the demonic spirits of the town. The experience with our youth work suggests to us that by removing the demonic spirit afflicting a place or area, we may well open the doors for evangelism. We realise that this in itself is not the total answer to taking the town for Christ, but we believe it is an important component in the process. We realise that this is also a progression not just in warfare but in holiness, both personal and corporate. Therefore it is conditional upon obedience. We ask that God will make us an obedient people.

Clive and Susie's group is at the sharp end of the strategy for warfare. It needs to be backed up by the prayers of the whole church, just as the front-line fighters of an army need support from the back-up troops.

The church at prayer

If the church is to go on the offensive in this whole matter of spiritual warfare, it is essential that, as far as possible, the whole church should be a church at prayer. If this is to happen it will take more than encouragement and calls to prayer. It will need structures to enable this to take place. We have instigated a network of prayer across the church, with each person praying for another two. There are also the specific prayer groups that meet regularly, and a group meets weekly before the family communion service.

The specific groups have their own areas of concern (eg, youth work). Each group is small enough to function as a unit with clear objectives which, we believe, have been set by the Lord. We say this because each one came into existence as the Lord pointed to the need.

Corporate fellowship

House groups are seen as units of warfare as well as of fellowship. They often provide not only the fellowship and pastoral care for the members, but also the ministry for healing and for release from demonic oppression. However, as far as the latter is concerned, we have a tight structure of oversight. All ministry that concerns the demonic must be referred to the leadership prior to such ministry taking place. It is then for the leadership to decide if ministry should take place in that context or some other. If it seems that more prayer back-up is required, then the spiritual warfare team is asked to assist. On other occasions it may be appropriate for the ministers themselves to be brought in. It is important that this ministry is undertaken with the full knowledge of those who have oversight because it is specifically to do with the authority of God and there is also a temptation to act in a covert manner wherever the demonic is involved.

All the structures and planning that we do come to naught if they are not God's plans. God wants to share his plans with us. He rejoices when we wish to work in partnership with him. Lack of co-operation and obedience are the main frustrations to the carrying out of God's plan. When we willingly co-operate there is a tremendous sense of his empowering, and this is usually a time when many come to know him. There has rarely been a time when people are more receptive to the gospel. Taking on strategic spiritual warfare will, we believe, open the doors for the gospel even more. It will require much higher levels of holiness and costly obedience, but there is a fabulous prize—the kingdom of heaven.

> Again the kingdom of heaven is like a merchant looking for fine pearls. When he found one of great value, he went away and sold everything he had and bought it (Mt 13:45–46).

9

The Spirit of The Age

What are people looking for in life today? What makes people tick? What is the basis of decision-making today? In other words, what is the spirit of our age?

Surely in attempting to find answers to these questions we are in danger of generalising and oversimplifying. Yet it is important to try because we need to see clearly what is happening around us. Since spiritual warfare has to be conducted in the real world, we have to understand what that is.

As we look back over the last few years, we expect we share the frustrations of many church leaders. Although we have seen many healed by the Lord, not all of them are still with us in church. Despite the tremendous blessings these people have received from God, somehow they do not remain with us. Of course there is nothing new in this; even when Jesus healed the ten lepers, only one came back: 'Jesus asked, "Were not all ten cleansed? Where are the other nine? Was no one found to return and give praise to God except this foreigner?"' (Lk 17:17–18).

What was the reason only one came back, and he a foreigner to boot? We are not told. Those men had a free choice to return to Jesus or not to do so. Their decision must have been based on the way they looked at life, on the pressing issues of the moment, and in the long term, on the spirit of the age.

One of the reasons we know that some have not stayed the course in the life of the church today is that we have failed to address ourselves to the spirit of the age. Sometimes we as a church simply do not realise what is going on in the lives and social situations of the people coming to God. We expect them to fit immediately into our framework and we fail to understand their real needs. As a result we leave people bereft, and do not minister in the power and love of Jesus to where they are.

It is very easy for a church to lose touch with the community which it is supposed to serve. This can be particularly true of growing churches. As renewal comes, the temptation is to create one's own church culture where everyone feels secure. Newcomers are required to jump an ever widening gulf between church and community. The church then rapidly loses the ability to relate to those outside its walls. The gospel is proclaimed, but in such a way that only those in the church can hear! The church then becomes marginalised, with little real effect on the community. Since those who manage to come to the Lord have to do a culture change, as well as come to know him, it may grow but only with like-minded people.

We have to be able to see with a clear eye where we are. We have to attempt to see the situation through the eyes of the Lord.

What is the spirit of the age?

It would certainly be unwise to make broad generalisations here. The world-view of those in high-income suburbia is probably different from that of people in more traditionally working-class areas. However, it is fair to assume that there will be common factors.

We realised that the place to find the spirit of the age was not in the church, but on the streets. We therefore asked our youth worker, Alex, to give us his thoughts and comments. He works mainly with those aged between sixteen and twenty-five and is based in the town centre of Tamworth. The vast majority of this age group do not have any higher education: they are employed in semi-skilled or unskilled jobs, or they are unemployed. There is, however, a college of further education in the town which attracts mostly local students. Tamworth is a young town, with lots of young families and vast numbers of young people.

They represent both this and the next generation. Their values will be passed on to their children and, to a large degree, they received their values from the previous generation. They are children of the Thatcher years. They are probably representative of the majority of young people in this country: only a few go to university, and only a few break out of the cultural framework that they are in. It is essential that we listen to them.

Alex

"People have not thought about the most basic of questions. On the street when I ask 'Does God care about you?', the responses are always vague:

'I suppose so.'

'Maybe.'

'Yeah, I guess he does.'

When I pushed a little harder by asking 'What do you think God is like?', the same people said:

'I don't believe in God.'

'He's everywhere.'

'He is a *******, my friend died two weeks ago in a motorbike crash.'

They are simply unaware of the contradictions in the statements. If you want a word for the spirit of the age it is 'unaware'. You get the sense that people are killing time and are simply unworried or oblivious of their mortality. Death is just a morbid Victorian relic, we do not need to bother with it.

There is little or no spiritual dimension to the age. People do not deny that it exists, they are just not particularly concerned. What spiritual thought there is, is a bit like a spiritual supermarket—a bit of this, a bit of that, all together, disjointed and contradictory!

The same person will accept there is no God, that death is the end, and that science can explain everything, while at the same time praying for God's protection, messing about with the occult, and having the firm belief that he will enter heaven!

In previous generations the mass of people were told what to believe. Now this is seen as wrong, as it prevents choice and free thinking. The net result, though, has not been to allow people to make up their own minds, but just unmade minds. The emphasis on multifaith teaching in schools has produced a pick-and-mix faith, if any!

Philosophical reason and logic are ignored. Christian witness based on reasoned argument is totally irrelevant. Contradictions in faiths are not deemed to be important. In themselves, people do not contradict themselves, but at different times utter views that are mutually exclusive. You can show them the inherent contradictions but the odds are it will be violently received, or rather, chucked back at you. If you believe something, it is true for you, that is all that matters. Why are you hassling me with your view? Leave me with mine."

Stress

On the 23rd September 1992 the BBC reported on the 6 o'clock news that the suicide rate for men aged between twenty-five and forty had gone up by twenty-five per cent since 1979. When the spokesperson for the Samaritans was asked for the cause of this, he said, 'Stress.'

In the Youth Hostel magazine *Triangle* (no 24 Summer 1992) a whole article, entitled 'The 90s Nightmare', was dedicated to the subject of stress in young people. It contained the following statement: 'We are not freaking out about AIDS, drug abuse and violence, we are panicking about our future and personal survival— financially, physically, psychologically and every other way.' Stress is no longer the prerogative of the company director, it is reaching into every part of our society.

It should be no surprise that when the pressure is on, for whatever reason, be it trauma, death in the family, or ill-health, the search for some kind of spiritual reality can take some very strange paths. There can no longer be the assumption that we are, at root, a Christian society. When the youth of the society do not see the church as being relevant when they need help, the very building-blocks of the Christian faith within our society have been removed.

For the church, the spirit of the age provides both condemnation and encouragement. It condemns because it sees the faith of the Christian as merely an alternative. Little remains to suggest that a Christian society is fundamental to life. The faith of the generation past has been largely discarded. The church is perceived as a dinosaur.

Barry Kissel, writing in the magazine *Anglicans for Renewal* (vol 50), had this to say:

> As I look across this land my greatest sadness is that our church has almost entirely lost my children's generation. To the twenty-year-olds what is presented to them as pertaining to God is to a large extent utterly irrelevant.
>
> I have ministered in the Church of England for twenty-five years. During that time we as an institution have never had the grace to admit our spiritual bankruptcy and desperate need to adopt the ways of Jesus and his Spirit.

If any one doubts the truth of these words, look at the local church. How many of the new generation are coming through? We are in a situation where there needs to be a radical rethink on every aspect of the church's life if we are to be a church that is true to the gospel, and wants to fulfil the Great Commission.

Yet this is also an encouraging time! The openness of the new generation is beyond belief at times. True, it is an openness that has limits, but it is an age in which people are free to hear. When the church is able to be free to proclaim the gospel in new ways that people can understand, remarkable things begin to happen.

The shackles of denominationalism are gradually falling off the church, facilitating a pooling of resources and a unity of message. The stakes at the present time are very high; the next generation is the prize.

At such a time as this, it should be of no surprise that the powers and principalities are at work. There is a mobilisation of demonic spiritual forces taking place across the globe, and at the same time, there is a flushing-out into the open of satanic activity. This is now being reported in the press, and several books have been written. For example, Peter Wagner in his book *Territorial Spirits* gives instances from all around the world.

To be channels of the gospel is going to mean getting involved in warfare. This, to a large extent, has been ignored in Britain. It can be no longer. To fail to

recognise the reality of the situation is to condemn our
children to a life of spiritual poverty and death.
Thankfully there is a growing awareness. At a conference
we attended recently, to our great surprise, it started
with prayer for dealing with these forces—great!

Who meets the spirit of the age?

If the church has, to a large extent, been unable to meet
the spirit of the age, there have been others who have
been willing to meet the challenge. The vacuum left by
the church is being filled. We are very subtly being
undermined and replaced. Stories involving mysterious
powers are fed to our children on television. Green issues
are high on the agenda, but we need to be wary of the
accompanying spirituality. The recent world summit
conference on the environment in Brazil (1992) was a
laudable event—at last world leaders were getting round
a table to discuss ways of conserving our environment;
but some delegates participated in the worship of Gaia,
the earth goddess of ancient Greek and Roman mythology.

The main attempt to fill the spiritual vacuum in the
West is coming from the so-called New Age movement.
It is much more widespread than people often give
credit. As we look round even a small market town like
Tamworth there are four shops stocking crystals in
various forms. They are often disguised as ornaments
with mythological figures holding them, but they are
there. No shop stocks something for which there is no
demand. We must look more closely at the New Age.

Why is the new age spreading?

New Age thinking is entirely acceptable to the pick-and-
mix kind of spirituality to which Alex referred. Any
attempt to define the New Age runs up against major

difficulties, as there are so many aspects to it. Indeed, it is not an organised movement at all, so even its title is a misnomer. Elliot Miller in his book *A Crash Course on the New Age Movement* (Monarch: 1990) describes it as a network: a vast, loosely related system, with many divergent strands, many sub-networks, with little superficial connection. You can pick and choose as you go along.

The *New Age Journal* stated back in 1982 (Lillie Wilson, New Age, vol 43 January 1982):

> ... the many issues of the new consciousness are like peanuts: you can't just eat one. The stockbroker for example, who began dabbling in alternative body therapies ten years ago has quite probably gone on to the likes of meditation or the ecology movement or Zen studies by now, and no doubt he notices the aperture in his personal cosmic egg getting wider all the time.

It is this ability to adapt to meet the needs of the spirit of the age that has resulted in the spread of New Age thinking. We need to listen to what is said because within it are the yearnings and the insights of this generation. Many of us would accept parts of the network, since they seem perfectly innocuous, and some of their crusades make us all sit up and think. We have to admit that the movement has put planet Earth and its conservation firmly on the world's agenda, and is troubling the consciences of world leaders and individuals alike.

In themselves, subjects such as concern for the environment, aromatherapy, or 'green' products can be quite acceptable. Certainly we should be concerned at the number of pills we pop down ourselves! Perhaps chewing liquorice bark is a good idea after all ... The difficulty lies not with the public appearance of the package, which is often in part commendable, but with the underlying assumptions that are part and parcel of it. Paul knew this dilemma intimately.

In 1 Corinthians 8 we find a discussion about eating the meat that has been sacrificed to idols. Paul argues that in itself meat is meat and has been created by God, and therefore is quite acceptable. It is possible to eat meat and not worship idols. However, if this creates a problem with your fellow-Christian, don't eat it!

Paul, of course, certainly would not agree with the worship of idols. Christians are often in the same dilemma with the New Age. We must be able to differentiate between the object and the belief system. Wholesale condemnation betrays prejudice and often disguises the real dangers. Having said that, it is true that one can lead to the other and this is the danger of which Paul warns. It is of particular concern where a person's hold on Christian belief is rather slender, but it is also true for non-Christians, and particularly for those who have a belief system which readily fits with the one on offer.

It is our experience that the New Age belief system is not neutral, and must be looked at very carefully, because the consequences of involvement are often far-reaching.

Main strands of belief in the New Age network

1. All is one. Everything that exists consists of the same reality. This is ultimate reality; it is being; it is awareness.
2. God and man are part of all this. So man is in reality divine.
3. Unfortunately, man is not often aware of this so he needs some spiritual mechanisms, such as meditation or chanting, to enable him to reach this awareness. The aim is to increase one's awareness that one's true self is God. Awareness is not an academic awareness, it

is experience. The touchstone is: do you feel it? Mystical experiences are doorways onwards, a personal transformation, an ongoing process. Experience, then, is the key. If it is not experienced then it is irrelevant. Authority is rooted in the individual and so it is what you or I experience that counts. It may not count for anyone else but that does not matter.

4. Most New Agers accept some form of the Hindu doctrines of reincarnation and karma. Karma says that whatever a person does, be it good or bad, will be repaid to him in the exact proportion next incarnation round. One needs several of these incarnations in order to get rid of the large amounts of bad karma, before you join the great reality and become part of it.

5. Evolution (what one does as an individual) is about the progression towards the attainment of one's true reality, which involves the increasing realisation and growth into the awareness that one is God. The more this is achieved, the more it affects not just oneself, but the whole world. In other words, there is a definite moving onwards that is important, not just for oneself but for everyone. The more people that seek to attain this reality, the better the world will be.

It should be clear that this does not tie in with orthodox Christianity—far from it. The way in which these doctrines are applied varies enormously, but the area that we have particularly come across is that of healing, and it is to this area we now turn.

Healing

In the last decade, many churches have rediscovered the God who heals in a real and sometimes dramatic way. It should be no great surprise that while this was happening, other forms of healing were becoming established. This process was accelerated by a growing dissatisfaction with the medical profession and the idea that if you are ill you throw a pill at it. Holistic remedies have come into vogue, and natural herb extracts, vitamins and the like have all become big business.

While the emphasis on 'natural' remedies may be applauded to a degree, there has also been a tremendous rise in 'spiritual' healing. Schools of healing have arisen, and centres set up in most countries around the world.

Is it Christian healing? For the Christian, several questions arise. How do we discover which are Christian healing groups? Is every group claiming to owe allegiance to Christ and to follow him therefore safe for a Christian to become involved with?

Suppose one is suffering from a persistent and painful illness which has been resistant to all medical treatment. One hears that a group which claims to engage in healing has been set up in the next town. How does one discern whether they really are Christian, and are safe to visit? We would like to suggest some preliminary questions which might help to solve this dilemma:

1. To what church do they belong? Who has authority and oversight over the group? To be a Christian is to belong to the body of Christ and to be subject, under God, to his given authority vested in the church. It does not always mean that a group is not Christian if they exist in isolation to the rest of the church, but it does suggest that one should proceed with great caution if no links exist with any recognised church.
2. Do they invoke only the Holy Spirit in the name of Jesus of Nazareth in their prayers and in their

ministry of healing? If they invoke and rely upon spirit guides, and if they heal in the name and in the power of departed spirits, they are not involved in the Christian healing ministry.

3. Which Christ do they believe in? That may seem a strange question. Surely there is only one. Well, yes there is, but he is perceived in astonishingly different ways by various groups. We would want to ask therefore: is he the Christ of the Bible and the mainstream churches? How do we discover?

- Jesus of Nazareth was born of Mary some 2,000 years ago and lived *only once* on earth. But some healing groups believe in a *Cosmic Christ* who has lived on earth several times. Some see him as a reincarnation of ancient gods, such as the Egyptian sun god.

- Do they believe in the saving power of the cross and that Christ died a cruel death in order to reunite us with our heavenly Father and provide a means for the forgiveness from our sins? Some healing groups evade the whole business of Christ's death on the cross. They spiritualise and sanitise it all. They 'soft pedal' on the whole issue of sin and forgiveness, and avoid it as far as possible.

- Do they major on spiritual healing? If so, who or what is the spiritual power? Do they speak of faith healing? Is the power in the supposedly gifted hands of the healer, or is it a direct gift of God, as indicated by Paul (1 Cor 12:9), to those who are prepared to be his servants and be used as channels of his love and healing?

- Do they speak of strange phenomena unheard of in the Bible? If you have never heard of the healing process or the spiritual condition before and you

cannot find reference to it in the pages of Scripture
—beware! Don't be impressed by technical language
or elaborate techniques.

- Do they believe in the neutrality of what they may
  describe as the 'spirit world'? Do they believe it is
  safe to commune with departed spirits? If so,
  beware! The Scriptures make it clear that the non-
  physical realm is not spiritually neutral, nor is it
  wholly good. The conflict with the powers of evil
  is as real there as it is here. As Christians, we believe
  in communing with God in prayer. The communication is with him, through Jesus, our only
  Mediator. All else is dangerous. We seek the
  guidance of the Holy Spirit and no other.
- Do they advocate loss of control of one's mind as
  part of the healing process—by the use of hypno-
  tism, trance, etc? Do they seek to heighten spiritual
  awareness by frequent repetition of a word or
  phrase—ie, do they use mantras? If so, be aware
  that these practices do not emanate from Christian
  teaching or the Christian healing ministry.
- Do they believe that the ultimate goal of mankind
  is to be so consumed by the inner light that one
  eventually overcomes mortality? In other words, is
  it the aim and purpose of all human striving to be
  assumed into, and become part of, the great reality?
  This is a far cry from the Christian belief in the
  resurrection of the dead and the life of the world
  to come.

Are these practices really just misguided and harmless
or do we need to be concerned about them? And what
about those 'healers' who do not claim to heal in the
name of Christ? Can any harm be done if they simply
seek to help and heal? It is impossible to generalise, but

the following account is a 'cautionary tale' which would suggest that extreme care should be exercised before seeking out a healer or a healing group.

Anne's story   Both John and Peter were involved in the ministry to Anne. She re-established contact with us because she was suffering from terminal cancer and was aware that the time was short. Anne was one of the most charming and open people we have met. She was one of the most spiritually thirsty and, due to her condition, was game to try anything if it brought hope of healing.

She very quickly came to see that Jesus was the only way, and became a committed Christian. She was a joy to be with as she had an open childlike faith. Yet her thirst for God in the years past had led her into some very strange places. She had tried as many spiritual approaches to healing as she could find, including meditating on an island with a mystic group, which apparently did not particularly help. She was prayed over by numerous 'healers', and felt no real progress had been made. Her search for the divine and for the filling of the aching void within her ended when she found Christ.

Mind you, she had had one or two frightening experiences on the way in her search for healing, particularly with spirit-guided experiences of what she was told were former incarnations of herself. She was led to believe that it was necessary to go into this if she was to be healed (presumably to try to find the cause of the cancer and deal with it). She related one such incident to Peter in which she saw herself in Egypt just about to be sacrificed to the sun god.

Anne was very honest. One day, during a time of prayer with John, she turned to him and said, 'John, I have a name buzzing around my head, I do not know it, I do not like it, and whenever I hear it an evil blackness overwhelms me. What does it mean?'

'What is it?' John asked.

Anne said, 'Beelzebub.'

At this point John became somewhat alarmed, but tried not to show it. He was aware that whatever was going on here was not minor. Beelzebub, in Mark 3:22, is called the 'prince of demons.' However, determined to claim the victory of Christ and her release from this recurring evil experience as quickly as possible, since her physical condition was giving concern, he laid his hand on Anne's head and told Beelzebub to go. Anne felt a dark cloud lift from her. John, on the other hand, felt strangely different—once again!

As he left the house, unreality started to descend. It was now about 7.30 in the evening. Unfortunately he could not get hold of Peter, as he was out at the time.

Peter got back home at about 10.15. The phone rang and a somewhat anguished John asked if Peter could please come down—now! When Peter learned what the situation was, his mother, who was visiting at the time, suddenly also found herself roped in. This required reinforcements.

John was in a bad way, slumped in the chair. He said he felt as though something had entered his skull and was literally and physically squeezing his brain. We came against Beelzebub in the name of Christ and John immediately recovered.

In retrospect it seemed that John had not taken even the most elementary precautions in his desire to deal with the situation immediately. There was no prayer back-up, he was ministering by himself, and as a result, had been taken out.

The more intriguing question, though, was where had this suddenly come from in Anne? There was no direct occultic involvement. The answer had to lie in her involvement with aspects of the New Age healing movement or other healers.

The New Age and the demonic

The vast majority of New Agers would emphatically deny that they have anything at all to do with the demonic. At one level that is probably true: the desire for world peace, the concern for wholeness, the awareness of environmental issues are all highly commendable. Yet they are dealing with matters from within their own world-view, as indeed Christians are with theirs. When you look at their beliefs and their view on life from a Christian world-view, there is much to cause concern.

Consistently there is a denigration of the Person and claims of Christ. Coupled with this there is a picking up and mixing of different belief systems, the result of which bears little resemblance to any one of the world faiths. This results, as far as Christianity is concerned, is a watering down of the claims of Christ. There is nothing new in this. It has happened at several points in history, but it has been consistently rejected by the Christian church.

To reach your divinity, in New Age thinking, you have to embark upon different types of spiritual techniques, which involve different meditative experiences. This is not neutral since much of it involves total spiritual openness, which, we would claim, can allow the infiltration of the demonic.

There are many different techniques on offer but the most common are types of meditation and exercise, yoga being one of them. The word 'yoga' means to yoke or to bind together. What is being bound together is the individual soul to the 'universal soul'. Is this universal soul the God of Christianity? If it is not, there are some serious questions to be asked. We believe that the universal soul cannot be called Christian, because:

1. Unity with the universal soul is by techniques, not by grace.
2. The teachings of yoga are rooted in ancient Hindu scriptures—the Upanishads, the Bhagavad Gita.

The argument that you can separate the practice—the physical exercise—from the original belief system, is flawed. One cannot say that doing exercises that were originally rooted in a religious belief system will not have an effect upon the spirit. From a Christian point of view, the death of Christ on the cross was a physical death, the resurrection of Christ was a physical resurrection. The coming of Christ as fully the Son of God in humanity points to the tremendous importance of the physical, and its close connection with the spiritual. It was not enough for Jesus resurrected to appear as a spirit to the disciples and particularly to Thomas. Thomas, for faith, had to physically touch Christ.

Elliot Miller (*A Crash Course on the New Age Movement*, p 94) reports the experiments of Harvard cardiologist Dr Herbert Benson. Benson attempted to administer his own meditative method in which he took out all religious connections. So instead of a mantra that used the name of a Hindu deity, he instructed patients to repeat the word 'one', a pleasant neutral word. Despite getting rid of as much religious association as possible, while retaining the exercise, the result was religious experience and conversion to eastern mysticism for some.

One could go on and look at the hundreds of different practices involved. Our great concern, though, is that part of New Age practice involves spiritual openness. Even coming for healing implies an openness to receive from the one doing the healing, but who is the source?

Our concern is that unwittingly we are seeing the spread of the demonic via this process. Anne's experience of Beelzebub points to this link. It is not conclusive, nothing ever will be, but Christians need to be aware, and seek to discern what is of Christ and what is not.

Added to the questions outlined above concerning healers, we now need to add a further one: do the spiritual techniques involved imply openness to, and the channelling of, an ambiguous force, or named force? If this is the case then there is a need to avoid it, because the possibility of demonic infiltration exists.

How should the church respond to the spirit of the age?

The spirit of the age demands immediacy and experience. It also requires a waiter service, with everything presented on a plate. There must be no stress involved, but there must be the promise of great things to come.

On the face of it, the Christian message does not sit easily with this. It is demanding and involves self-sacrifice, and yet it is full of love and care. There is, however, an immediacy about the Lord's dealings with us which can be actually experienced. He wants to reach into the pain and hurt of people's lives. He wants to heal and he wants to bring about repentance. Our experience in the healing ministry is that God so often responds in an instant as people come in trust seeking his help. When John prayed recently with a girl who had been abused, God's response was immediate. She arrived shivering with cold and yet, in a moment, she was bathed in God's love and warmth when they prayed. So much so, she had to take her coat off! It was the first step of her healing.

The church needs to rediscover the immediacy of God. The world about us is impatient with a church that fails to see this. They perhaps know it intuitively and despair of a church which fails to see what is staring it in the face.

We need to hear God anew, or to put it another way, there is a crying need for a prophetic church: a church that can see what God wants and responds. The spirit of the age is not interested in fine theories or reasoned argument, it needs to know and experience God—now.

The people of God must be a prophetic and obedient people in the ordinary things of life. If, for instance, they are walking down the street and they become aware that God wants to touch the person passing, they should be prepared to do it.

For too long the emphasis has been on the pastoral nature of the church. Ministers are actually called 'pastors'. At worst, this has reduced the church to the level of a mutual massage parlour. At best it has produced fine pastoral care but limited growth. The church is to be led and empowered. The disciples were told by Jesus not to do anything until they received the Holy Spirit. There is no substitute for this.

Until the church picks up the prophetic mantle and seeks to discover in a consistent and thoroughgoing way what God wants, it will not move out in the power of God. This is not a recipe for triumphalism—quite the reverse. It needs the recognition of our own spiritual bankruptcy, it is based on our own poverty, so that we can receive the power and love of Christ: 'Blessed are you who are poor, for yours is the kingdom of God' (Lk 6:20).

It is as we move out of the bunker that the warfare starts. The fight is against the principalities and powers, not against flesh and blood. This is the reality. We pray that the church will wake up to this fact.

10

The Nature of Victory

In early December 1992 the BBC *Panorama* programme produced a documentary on satanic ritual abuse. It was wide-ranging and looked at the possibility of child sacrifice; and the existence of the demonic. The programme paid particular attention to the nature of evidence given by children. The general conclusions were that in the USA this whole issue has reached the point of near-hysteria. They highlighted the danger that this was beginning to spread into Britain.

We thoroughly agree that there is a need to be realistic and have one's feet firmly on the ground in this matter. However, the programme gave the impression that all talk of the demonic and the satanic was 'over the top'. It is very difficult to keep a clear perspective, and the tendency to jump to extremes must be avoided. The programme, however, jumped to one extreme, while many jump to the other.

We would love to join the ranks of those who say that this whole area is total nonsense. If we never had to deal with another curse, or get involved with another deliverance, it would be a great relief! Unfortunately, life is not like that. We write from the viewpoint of personal experience, not of evidence which would stand up in a court of law.

In early January 1993, we were sitting at the computers editing this book together. Dual authorship has its pains as well as its joys! We had started at about 10am and our mood was somewhat light-hearted as we joked about this and that. Suddenly after about an hour we heard two large cracks! They sounded as though two high-voltage wires had touched together. This quickly sobered our mood. Was someone, we wondered, taking pot-shots at us? Carefully Peter edged round the outside of the vicarage to look at the wall of the room where we were working. Not a mark was to be seen. Two over-excited imaginations, perhaps? The cracks continued throughout the day, moving around the room, and getting louder as the day wore on. It wasn't electrical, as far as we could see and there seemed to be no explanation. We continued the editing and came to one of the chapters that deals with ministry. Confusion and emotional pain suddenly overwhelmed us. It was getting very difficult to see the computer screens. When we came to the end of the chapter the strange symptoms lifted. We felt fine and back to normal, so we carried on.

At about 4pm, one of John's sons came into the room. 'Blimey!' he said. 'This place stinks like an open sewer.'

Now perhaps one of us had a personal hygiene problem, but the funny thing was that neither of us had smelt a thing. This was the third time that someone had commented on the smell of sewage in the room where we were writing. There are no main drains on that side of the house.

We were not entirely clear what was happening, but certainly something was. We prayed over the room, ourselves and the computers. The possibility occurred to us that high levels of static discharge could perhaps be the cause. Then came the awful thought that the computer discs might be damaged. They weren't.

It has not been a particularly enjoyable experience writing this book. We have both had our weak areas afflicted by curses. We have had to face considerable pain within and bring it before the Lord and one another for healing. The result is that we are moving towards wholeness. Certainly it has been a 'school of pain'. We sense that God has allowed this to happen because he wants a holy people who can be more effective for him. He doesn't want us dragged down by our own pain. He wants us free to hear his agenda, not the agenda set by our own needs.

The nature of faith

In Mark 5:25–34, Jesus' cloak is touched by the woman who was bleeding. When she touched his cloak she was made whole. We are told that: 'At once Jesus realised that power had gone out from him' (v 30). Jesus turned to the woman and said, 'Daughter, your faith has healed you. Go in peace and be freed from your suffering' (v 34).

Faith had healed her because faith galvanised her to go to the source of healing, which was Jesus. Clearly she assented to the fact that Jesus could heal, but more was needed than that. She had to touch his cloak. Faith is not a commodity to be owned but a dynamic trust that prompts action. Until faith operates in action it is simply assent to truth.

This perhaps is best seen in the feeding of the five thousand (Mk 6:30–44). Jesus broke the five loaves and two fishes and handed them out to the disciples. What was going on in the minds of the disciples? If we were faced with hundreds of hungry people and a couple of measly bits of bread and the tail of a fish, what would our response be? When Jesus blessed the bread and fish, hefty baskets of fish and bread did not suddenly descend

from the skies! Our response would probably have
ranged from 'how long will it take me to run away?' to
one of trust. Perhaps the response of the disciples was
a bit of both. Even they must have had that nasty sinking
feeling when Jesus asked them to take the bread and
fish to the people. The miracle happened in the giving
out of the bread and fish. The point when assent turned
to dynamic faith which says 'yes' to Jesus' direction was
the point when they obediently moved into action.

For many of us this is highly uncomfortable; we much
prefer 'armchair-safari' Christianity. We can experience
all the thrills and joys at a safe distance and it does not
actually involve us in any risky ventures. Unfortunately
it also bars us from the reality of victory. We can quote
all the Scripture we want but it has no meaning beyond
assent unless we move out in faith, and it certainly does
not disturb Satan.

For the disciple Peter, the discovering of this truth was
a wet experience. In Matthew 14:22–32, Peter is called
by Jesus to walk on the water:

> But when he saw the wind, he was afraid and, beginning to
> sink, cried out 'Lord save me!' Immediately Jesus reached
> out his hand and caught him. 'You of little faith,' he said,
> 'why did you doubt?' (vv 30–31).

Walking on water means that we have to keep our eyes
on Christ. It is an uncomfortable experience learning
how to do this, and we often get wet. Yet it has been our
experience that God honours even the smallest steps of
faith, and catches us when we fall. We have to learn by
stepping out and falling, just like a toddler trying to walk,
and it applies to all forms of Christian ministry including
spiritual warfare. However, like the toddler learning to
walk under the supervision of a parent, where it is safe
to fall, so for us the learning process must be made safe,

so others do not get hurt. This is best done by learning with those who are experienced in such ministry.

We have often fallen and will no doubt continue to do so. It is interesting to note that Peter started to sink because of fear. Why was this? It turned him away from faith and so away from Christ. The main strategy of the demonic attack on the church is to cause fear, and so provoke a similar response to that of Peter.

Faith means we have to decide. We all have a choice to make: are we going to stay in the armchairs enjoying a second-hand experience of the victory of the few, or are we going to get up and move out? Faith means in or out, it is either in action or not. To get up and move out means that our entire security has to be placed in Jesus, and nothing else.

Unfortunately we may have to learn the hard way, since we all invest our security primarily in other things, people, and family. Those securities will be exposed if we decide to walk, and it will be painful; our weak areas will be shown up for what they are. The uncompromising reality of walking with Jesus shows up our weaknesses. It does not allow for comfortable sins or self-delusion. Of course the Lord is very gentle with us, but he loves us too much to turn a blind eye. This is the dual message of the gospel and it is set out clearly in Romans 8:17: 'Now if we are children, then we are heirs—heirs of God and co-heirs with Christ, if indeed we share in his sufferings in order that we may also share in his glory.'

Christ's sufferings were because of our sin and for no other reason. We are co-heirs with Christ 'if indeed . . .' we accept the role of heirs of God, which is to share in the sufferings of Jesus as well as his glory. To share in the sufferings of Christ is to share in the pain of sin. This is, in part, our own sin, as we put to death by the Spirit the misdeeds of the body (Rom 8:13). To do this is to suffer as we face the pain inside. It also involves sharing the ridicule and pain of standing with Jesus in a hostile world, before sharing the glory of being children who 'fought the good fight'. Far too often we are selective in the use of this verse and we conveniently omit the part about sufferings. We present a soft-option gospel. In our evangelism we often enhance this myth, by presenting the gospel as the answer to all ills (which it is), but we forget to tell people about the cost. If we face the sufferings we will also share in his glory, that is the promise and the choice.

The victory

Victory which is acknowledged solely by assent is not victory. Victory only becomes a reality when assent grows into faith in action. Of course there has to be assent before faith. The two have to go together.

There is a problem in moving from assent to faith, and the problem is fear. Fear jams the movement. Unfortunately, sometimes people get stuck halfway, paralysed by fear. In the area of spiritual warfare this can be very common and the result is that people give undue credence to the demonic, see demons under beds and so on. This happens particularly with those who are naturally fearful. It takes great gentleness, encouragement and the love of God to bring people through.

How can victory be reality?

Assent We need to know what the Bible says, we need to understand what happened on the cross. Watchman Nee in his book *Sit, Walk, Stand* (Kingsway: 1962, pp 43–44) points out that all the weapons in Ephesians 6 are defensive, except perhaps for the sword, which can be. So we are not trying to gain the ground: it is already ours, because of Jesus' victory on the cross—every other claim is bogus. Today we war against Satan only to maintain and consolidate the victory which Jesus has already gained. By the resurrection God has proclaimed his Son Victor over the whole realm of darkness, and the ground Christ won he has given to us.

So our task is to claim what is rightfully God's in his name. If we think in terms of taking Satan's ground, we have got the wrong picture, the victory has been won by Christ, so it is already ours, because we are his children.

Suffering The difficulty of facing up to sin, our own and others, results in suffering. Strangely this is more difficult for many who have been Christians for years. The reason for this is that many of us, particularly leaders, have been given a cheap doctrine of repentance. Often we have been schooled to think that repentance is saying sorry, and trying not to do it again. This rarely happens; we sin again and again, in the same area. Now up to a point this is going to be a regular experience, since we will not be fully healed until we reach heaven. Indeed it was the experience of Paul: 'I do not understand what I do. For what I want to do I do not do, but what I hate I do' (Rom 7:15).

Yet this is in contrast to his statement in Romans 6:18: 'You have been set free from sin and have become slaves to righteousness.'

Paul's experience reflects the tension we all know. It is true that we have been set free, yet it is a freedom that is coming into being. A cheap doctrine of repentance allows for continual sin as a routine cycle without much hope of a change. It does not allow for real repentance which is a radical turn round. Actual turning around means facing the root causes of sin, facing who we really are, and facing the pain in doing so.

Anger, jealousy, rejection, love and joy are the basic human-building blocks with which we must deal if this process is to be worked through. Barth rightly said that religion is the enemy of a real relationship with God, because religion can hide the base motives and feelings which we all have.

So for example, if one happens to see a beautiful girl to whom one is strongly sexually attracted and wants to get her into bed, the realities of the situation can be smothered in a false religious piety. One knows lust is wrong, so one rejects those feelings and convinces oneself that one is really attracted to her because God created all beauty and one must therefore admire God's handiwork! This is religious cuckooland. Unless the reality of lust is faced, how can there be true repentance?

The attack on the church is allowed by God in order that the holiness of the church can develop. It means facing the basic instincts, it means facing and taking responsibility for who we are in ourselves, then bringing the real me for healing. This process inevitably involves suffering.

This process is essential for living in the victory. To duck the pain of our sin is to nullify in our lives the reality of the victory. To see the victory is to face the pain, surrounded in the love of God, and bring out real repentance. If this process is real and honest the victory is real.

The glory   '. . . that we may also share in his glory' (Rom 8:17). The glory of Christ is that of being the Son of the Father. The glory that is given to us, as our inheritance, is to be sons and daughters of the Father. This is a glory beyond comparison. It makes available all the resources of the Father to further his kingdom. These resources of power and love are of such consequence that nothing can stand against us, not even Satan.

One of the comments that we heard from those coming out of satanism is that they could not attack men and women of God who were obedient to him. The power and the love of God mean that there is no contest.

The seventy-two returned with joy and said 'Lord, even the demons submit to us in your name.'

He replied, 'I saw Satan fall like lightning from heaven' (Lk 10:17–18).

The Believer's Guide To Spiritual Warfare

by Tom White

How to resist the devil through hand-to-hand combat in the spiritual realm.

What is spiritual warfare, and who should be engaged in it?

How do we join battle? What are our weapons?

Tom White made a pledge to God when he became a Christian that he would help others remain free of the Enemy that nearly destroyed his life. *The Believer's Guide to Spiritual Warfare* will help you to:

- deal with oppression
- resist temptation
- pray effectively for your family
- break curses
- cleanse places
- distinguish the demonic from the psychological, emotional and physical

and much, much more.

'Those who take Satan seriously, and the victory of Jesus even more seriously, would be well advised to take this book seriously as well.'

PETER LAWRENCE
Vicar of Christ Church,
Burney Lane, Birmingham

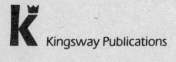

Kingsway Publications

Dance With The Devil

by Audrey Harper

She was the devil's dancing partner, and he wasn't going to let her go without a stuggle.

For years Audrey carried a dark secret. Anyone could see she was a drug addict; some knew about the stealing and the degrading life she'd led. But she could tell no one, not even those closest to her, about the coven and the horrors she had witnessed there.

Now Audrey tells her story, providing evidence of the reported rise in ritual and sexual abuse among adults and children today. The cold fear that once held her in the depths of misery has gone. *Dance with the Devil* reveals why, and offers hope to those influenced by satanism—as well as help to those who fight against it.

'The occult is hurting so many—including children. Audrey's honest and powerful story helps us to hear the cries of the victims and to understand what is really going on.'
—**KEVIN LOGAN**,
author of *Paganism and the Occult*

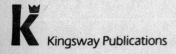

Kingsway Publications

Deliverance Means Love

by Audrey Harper

The Enemy has many strings to his bow. He will use every circumstance of life to draw people away from the truth and destroy their minds, their emotions, their very lives. Homelessness, unemployment, boredom, peer pressure or just human weakness can all be doorways—particularly for young people—into the false promises of the occult.

What can ordinary Christians do to deliver from evil those most at risk?

Audrey Harper wrote in her first book, *Dance with the Devil*, about her own rescue from satanism, and she knows that deliverance means love above anything else we can do. Here she gives down-to-earth suggestions that will strengthen our churches as havens for victims of the occult, so presenting a continuing threat to the devil's strategy.

'From vagrant to platform speaker, Audrey's experiences carry a sometimes uncomfortable message to the church. She is gifted with a down-to-earth manner, a mischievous sense of humour, but above all a burning compassion for people to discover the love of Jesus through his church.'

—CLIVE CALVER
General Director, Evangelical Alliance UK

'In a day when most books are about living "successful" Christian lives, we must ask the question: who will accept the failures? Who will give them the atmosphere of love, trust and discipline they need? This is what Audrey Harper is seeking to do, and this is the message of her book. Reachout Trust is glad that there are people like Audrey.'

—DOUG HARRIS
Reachout Trust

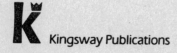

Kingsway Publications

Devil On The Run

by Nicky Cruz

'I did not realise that I had the curse of my forefathers. The evil my father practised was destined for me.'

Nicky's parents made their living from the occult. The people of Puerto Rico came from miles around for exorcism, healing and fortune telling. One of eighteen children, he grew up with an intimate knowledge of the reality of the spirit world—and aware that he was to follow in his parents' footsteps.

Nicky was the black sheep of the family. Yet, as a gang leader in New York, he was the first in his family to turn to Christ.

In the course of his long ministry as an evangelist, Nicky has seen many manifestations of Satan's power—and the defeat of that power through Christ. He graphically describes these battles, and the threats that face our sceptical world.

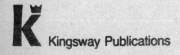

Kingsway Publications